INTERORGANIZATIONAL RELATIONS
IMPLICATIONS FOR COMMUNITY
DEVELOPMENT

INTERORGANIZATIONAL RELATIONS
Implications for Community Development

Charles L. Mulford
Iowa State University, Ames, Iowa

Volume IV, Center for Policy
Research Monograph Series

Series Editor: Amitai Etzioni

HUMAN SCIENCES PRESS, INC.
72 FIFTH AVENUE
NEW YORK, N.Y. 10011

Copyright © 1984 by Human Sciences Press, Inc.
72 Fifth Avenue, New York, New York 10011

Printed in the United States of America
123456789

Library of Congress Cataloging in Publication Data

Mulford, Charles L.
  Interorganizational relations.

  (Center for Policy Research monograph series,
ISSN 0731-809X ; v. 4)
  Includes bibliographies and index.
  1. Interorganizational relations.   2. Community
development.   3. Interorganizational relations—United
States—Case studies.   I. Title.   II. Series.
HM 131.M794   1982   302.3'5   83-18616
ISBN 0-89885-147-5

To Mary,
Dave and Katy

CONTENTS

Chapter 3. THE EXTERNAL RELATIONS OF PARTICULAR
ORGANIZATIONS: STRATEGIES FOR MANAGING
ENVIRONMENTS

PREFACE

Lay persons, administrators, leaders, and specialists have increasingly come to recognize the crucial impact that interorganizational relations (IOR) have on our lives. This book presents a comprehensive analysis of the nature and consequences of IOR. The community is portrayed as a system of relations in the first chapter. Alternative units of analysis and key dimensions are presented in the second chapter. The external relations of particular organizations, with an analysis of strategies used to manage their environments, are presented in Chapter 3. Dyadic relations are analyzed in Chapter 4. Relations between boundary spanners, those persons who represent and negotiate for their organizations, and constraints on the behavior of boundary spanners are covered in the fifth chapter. The mobilization of networks is presented in Chapter 6. Specific contributions to community development and planning are reviewed and summarized in Chapter 7.

One cannot but be struck by the rapid expansion of knowledge about IOR that has occurred in the past decade. We have learned a great deal about why, how, and with what consequences organizations relate to each other. Nevertheless, conceptual and empirical gaps remain. In particular, applications for practitioners are incomplete. These and other priority issues and unresolved problems are considered by persons with diverse backgrounds in Chapter 8.

I have made deliberate efforts to specify relevant points for practitioners in each chapter. Discussion questions, suggested activities, and cases are provided at the end of each chapter for application and to encourage the reader to gain subject matter depth. The discovery of IOR has been particularly exciting for me. I hope that this book will help encourage practitioners to learn more about and use an interorganizational perspective in their work and I hope that specialists who share my enthusiasm will find this book helpful in their work.

ACKNOWLEDGEMENTS

Many people have helped me in a variety of ways in the development and preparation of this book. Students in my graduate classes have read drafts of chapters, critiqued my thinking, and shared ideas with me. Iowa State University granted me a faculty improvement leave during 1980 to write, and the Graduate College provided some funds for typing. Linda Arends and Georgia Parham typed the chapters, offered many helpful suggestions, and most patiently made corrections.

Gerald Klonglan, who is the chairperson of sociology, offered helpful suggestions, helped me obtain the leave for writing, and most importantly expressed enthusiasm for this book's development. I would also like to thank colleagues in my department, especially Harry Cohen and Patricia Keith, who have encouraged my efforts. I am very grateful to my colleagues who have read this book and prepared sections for the final chapter, namely, Betty Wells, Vern Ryan, Richard Hall, Joe Molnar, and Steven Paulson.

I am also grateful to Diana Pounds and Pat Kinney of the *Ames Tribune* for allowing me to excerpt news articles for the case for chapter 6. I have been most fortunate to have had Debbie Wells working with me as a research assistant during 1981–1982. Debbie has assisted with library research, read and critiqued chapters, assisted in editorial work, and offered suggestions with regard to this book's format. Debbie's help is most gratefully acknowledged.

Last, but not least, I would like to express my thanks to the many research subjects, agency administrators, and lay persons who have shared their experiences about IOR with me and who have helped me grow and develop professionally.

Chapter 1

THE COMMUNITY AS A SYSTEM OF INTERORGANIZATIONAL RELATIONS

INTRODUCTION

It is commonplace today to speak about the importance of organizations for us personally and for our community. Open your purse or billfold for a moment. If a detective were looking at the contents, how much of your identity could he construct? How much could he learn about what is important for you from the membership cards, credit cards, and other evidence linking you to organizations? I sometimes ask people during the first day of class to exchange purses or billfolds and to use the contents to develop a profile of the "stranger" next to them. The evidence clearly shows how important organizations are for us. Pick up any newspaper or magazine or listen to any television show for a few minutes. It is nearly impossible to find a single news story or hear about a single current event without connecting it with some organization.

Most of the important events in our lives have happened and will happen in organizations. Many of us were born in a hospital, we went to school, attend a church or synagogue, work for an organization, belong to a union or professional organization to protect our jobs, participate in leisure or recreation sponsored by organizations, and support a political party. We turn to organizations when we think about the correction of a social problem or realize that our community is facing a crisis. Organizations are needed for our personal growth and survival, and organizations are absolutely essential for collective efforts.

It is relatively easy to recognize the importance of organizations, but what we are beginning to become increasingly aware of today is that the nature and scope of interorganizational relations (IOR) provide another crucial dimension for our existence. More and more in recent years, citizens, social critics, political leaders, corporate executives, and researchers have shown increased concern for relationships between organizations.

It is virtually impossible for ordinary citizens to be unaware of the importance of IOR. To illustrate this point, pretend for a few minutes that you are riding in an auto or on a bus with John Doe on the way to work in a typical community. A glance at the morning paper angers John Doe. One story points out the lack of cooperation between two social service agencies in the community that serve common clients. A second story warns of the continued threat of hostility between the United States and another country. Oh well, the Yankees won again; there is some good news! And the state university, John Doe's alma mater, has been successful in getting increased funding for new programs and buildings from the legislature.

As John Doe gets off the bus, he notices people walking around the building carrying signs that say "On Strike" and wonders if the strike will affect the company. Once inside the office, things begin to look brighter again. The employment agency calls to tell John Doe that they have found several well-qualified applicants for the job opening in his section. Then the good news really arrives. The morning mail includes a letter from the federal agency with which he has been in contact. The federal contract has just been signed and the new project can be started. He begins to think immediately about contacting subcontractors and other firms that will be involved. All in all, it really does promise to be a good day! And look at how much of the day's events and actions have involved relationships between organizations. In fact, it would be nearly impossible to fully appreciate this or any typical day for John Doe without understanding the role played by relationships between organizations.

In their observation about the importance of understanding bureaucracies, Blau and Meyer (1971, pp. 10–16) stated there were reasons that made this understanding more important than ever. We should have an understanding of bureaucratic organizations because they are so prevalent and provide so many services for us. In addition, an understanding of bureaucracy is required for citizens in a democracy if they are to influence governmental bodies and agencies. Social scientists are interested in bureaucratic organizations because they are natural laboratories for social research.

Paraphrasing Blau and Meyer, it is becoming increasingly necessary for us to understand the nature and consequences of IOR for practical, ideological, and scientific reasons. We have already observed how the lives of citizens are touched in many ways by IOR.

Social critics and those concerned with community problems increasingly discuss these problems in terms of IOR. William Reid (1964) has observed that a lack of coordination between social service agencies can be seen as a major constraint on deliquency prevention and control efforts. Reid (1975) stated that a lack of coordination existed for the most part in all areas of social welfare. Clark (1965) has discussed IOR in education. Attention has also focused upon the health delivery system, manpower services, juvenile justice system, social service programs, community decision organizatons, and county and state level planning agencies (Aldrich, 1976; Hall, 1972; Molnar and Rogers, 1979; Warren, 1971). These research projects have been concerned with existing relationships between organizations, with resulting consequences for clients, the organizations themselves, and the wider community.

Political leaders at all levels of government who must establish program priorities, assess budget requests, and even eliminate some programs encourage coordination between agencies in hopes of reducing waste and duplication. Sometimes funding is made available only when agencies agree to coordinate some aspects of their programs, and coordination sometimes is even mandated.

Why do business leaders show so much interest in IOR? Business leaders may find it to their advantage to pool their available capital for joint business ventures that would not otherwise be possible. A business organization that is too dependent upon a single market for its products or services may try to diversify in order to loosen its dependency.

Vertical corporate mergers are used by corporations in order to control all relevant activities from the acquisition of raw materials to production and marketing. Some corporate mergers occur in order to help the participants gain additional capital and expertise. Multinational corporations are effective because they have developed relationships with many other corporations in different countries.

Today social scientists clearly recognize that organizations are constrained by their environments and that other organizations are among the most important elements in an organization's environment. Organizations influence each other because they are interdependent. If transactions between organizations are repeated and relationships persist, we speak in terms of the emergence of "community structure." Changes in the environment that call for the development of new relationships or decisions by organizational leaders to use different strategies to manage their environment can, in turn, lead to changes in community structure.

Social scientists are also interested in IOR because this knowledge shows promise of aiding in the development of an alternative model of the community. Hopefully, this new model will allow us to avoid some of the conceptual pitfalls faced by traditional models.

IOR AND COMMUNITY STRUCTURE

Traditional models of community have come under severe attack and some critics question if the models were *ever* applicable. Even the assumptions associated with traditional models have been questioned (for example, see Bates and Bacon, 1972; Sanders, 1966; Warren, 1963; Young and Larson, 1965).

Young and Larson (1965) were among the first to call for a different way of viewing communities. Traditional approaches that rely heavily upon household surveys, they argued, tell us little about "community" as an organized structure of social meaning and relationships rather than as just a collection of individuals. Organizations serve as a frame of reference with which members can make sense out of their activity and environment. Knowledge about patterns of relationships is essential for understanding community. This perspective permits analysis of dimensions not possible through the study of individuals alone. Young and Larson also indicated that communities within communities can be analyzed with the interorganizational perspective. Even spatially separate organizations can be considered a part of "community" if they are included in a particular hierarchy or network.

Bates and Bacon (1972) observe that sociologists have been very well aware of how ill-defined and imprecise is the traditional concept of community. Humanistic assumptions about community have led some to think that communities consist only of people and concrete biological families; romantic assumptions have emphasized that cooperation reigns over all other social processes most of the time and that conflict is relatively rare and dysfunctional.

Bates and Bacon join ranks with others (Bernard, 1973; Warren, 1963; Young and Larson, 1965) who have severely questioned the geographic assumption of community. Do readily defined geographic boundaries of communities exist? Do political and jurisdictional lines really establish meaningful boundaries? These critics argue that while there still may be "local" attachment for many when persons think about community, clearly defined geographic boundaries are not needed for all analytic purposes. Bertrand (1972, p. 155) indicates that to determine community boundaries or the boundaries of subsystems within the community one must determine which groups and organizations interact most frequently and/or intensively in the fulfillment of life needs.

Units of Analysis

The subsystem, which is the basic unit of community analysis, can be anlayzed in terms of its structure of network of organizations (Sanders, 1966; Warren, 1963). Sanders (pp. 170–172) has pointed out that community studies become sociological only when they begin to trace the social networks that exist. Even beginners can easily learn of these networks, which are revealed as follows:

1. when one traces the wide variety of statuses and roles that a single individual may fulfill during the course of his daily activity;

2. by concentrating not on single individuals but on the study of a sample of groups and organizations in the community; or

3. by describing how the members of a community are organized to meet some recurring need.

Units of analysis smaller than subsystems include particular organizations, organizational sets, and interorganizational collectivities (ICs). A particular organization's input set includes those organizations upon which it is dependent for resources and the output set includes the organizations receiving or distributing its products or services (Evan, 1965). Interorganizational collectivities range from dyads to larger networks. We will see in Chapter 2 that considerable work needs to be completed in specifying the proper comparative and relational properties for analyzing collectivities (Marrett, 1971).

Organizations cannot exist alone since they are not self-sufficient, do not represent specialized action systems, and perform only part of the total behavior necessary for the system. Interdependencies make for uncertainty in decision making because they may lead to the necessity of increased coordination and mutual control over each other's activities. Pfeffer and Salancik (1978, pp. 44–46) have summarized the factors that increase the likelihood of an organization complying with control attempts by another organization and factors that are critical in determining the dependence of organizations on each other. We will see later when we look in depth at ICs that balanced or symmetric relationships (the organizations are mutually dependent) are less likely to lead to conflict than asymmetric dependencies.

"Interstitial organizations" (Bates and Bacon, 1972, p. 377) play a crucial role in promoting exchanges and coordination in the community and in reducing the negative effects of conflict. Interstitial organizations contain representatives of other organizations. For example, the chamber of commerce manages relations between potentially conflicting organizations. Voluntary organizations, civic clubs, and community planning and action groups have long been the focus of community research, and Bates and Bacon point out that all are interstitial organizations. This means that an increase or decrease in the number, scope, and potency of these coordinative interstitial organizations constitutes an important aspect of community dynamics.

Horizontal and Vertical Linkages

The distinction must be made between relationships involving units at the same level and relationships with units at more inclusive levels. Warren (1963, pp. 237–302) uses the term "horizontal dimension" to refer to relationships with units at the same level and "vertical dimension" refer to relationships with units at a more inclusive level. Relationships between collectivities within a community contribute to a community's horizontal pattern and relationships with organizations at county, state, or federal levels would contribute to a community's vertical pattern. The "great change" in American communities is thought in part to relate to the weakening of the horizontal pattern in the typical community, the strengthening of its vertical pattern, and the acceptance of this by citizens as they look to the state or federal government to solve their problems (Warren, 1963, pp. 237–266).

Comprehensive Focus on the "Field"

Warren (1967, p. 397) has pointed out that the overall "field," or patterned network within which organizations interact, has a great impact on the interaction between organizations.

Warren cites the example of how two department stores will relate to each other if there are only two compared to how they will relate if they are but two of twenty in a community. The concept of fields are relevant for subsystems and for the community, too. Unfortunately, very little research has been completed on IOR fields.

Turk (1970; 1973) has led the way in the empirical analysis of networks found in 130 U.S. cities of more than 100,000 population. For certain purposes the characteristics of the field can be used to predict other characteristics of the same situation without regard to more conventional units of analysis such as individuals and role categories. For example, Turk (1973, p. 37) has proposed that the establishment of formal relationships among a set of organizations depends upon the system's capacity and need for such relationships. Turk found that the scale and diversity of municipal government and of community-wide voluntary associations were more important in the formation of hospital councils than any other variables. We will look much closer at Turk's pioneering studies and will also become familiar with such innovative methodologies as network analysis that are being developed (for example, see Galaskiewicz, 1979).

DYNAMICS OF GENERAL AND SPECIFIC ENVIRONMENTS

According to Katz and Kahn (1978, p. 122), with the exception of the organization under study at a particular time, everything else in the universe has been treated under the rubric of "environment." More adequate conceptualization of environment and more empirical research is needed for us to better understand the community as a system of IOR.

Hall (1977, pp. 303–332) defines the environment as the general and specific influences on organizations. General environmental conditions must be of concern to all organizations. While specific organizations must respond to those general conditions that are most relevant, the conditions are the same for all. General environmental conditions include technological, political, economic, demographic, ecological, and cultural conditions. Specific environmental conditions have to do with other organizations with which an organization directly interacts or particular individuals crucial to the organization.

The specific environment has also been called the task environment (Thompson, 1967, pp. 27–28) or the relevant environment (Dill, 1958). The task environment of an organization concerns those parts of the environment that are relevant or potentially relevant for goal setting and goal attainment. The relationship between an organization and its task environment is principally one of exchange (Thompson, 1967, pp. 28–29). Dill has stated that task environments of business firms include:

1. customers,
2. suppliers of materials, labor, capital, equipment, and work space,
3. competitors, and
4. regulatory organizations and agencies.

With appropriate modification this scheme can be used to discuss the task environment of any organization. The reader should note that Evan's (1965) concept of "organization set" is a related but more limited concept than task environment because the task environment includes all organizations that have actual or potential influence on the focal organization.

Conceptions of Environment

Two ways of conceptualizing the environment have been discerned: the environment as a pool of needed resources and the environment conceptualized as information (Aldrich, 1979; Aldrich and Mindlin, 1978). When the environment is treated as resources available, the key concept is dependence, or related concepts including resource exchange, relative power, control over sources of support, and the impact of transactions on organizational structure.

The information conception refers to the acquisition of information about elements in the external system and relies heavily upon theories of perception and decision making. Uncertainty for decision makers is the basic concept used by investigators when the environment is treated as the flow of information.

These two perspectives on environment correspond with the objective-subjective environment classification scheme sometimes seen in organizational literature. The term "objective" usually refers to tabulations of objects or events in an organization's environment by an observer or researcher, whereas the term "subjective" has reference to measures that tap organizational members' perceptions of their organizations' environments (Downey and Ireland, 1979). Organizational analysts tend to adopt either the resources (objective) conception of environment or the information (subjective) conception.

The key concepts from both dimensions, resource dependency on the environment and relative uncertainty, are important. Aldrich (1979) proposes that dependence alone may not be as critical as when it is combined with uncertainty. In other words, the most threatening situation for an organization is to be dependent upon others and relatively uncertain about what the future holds. If we wear our conceptual blinders to focus only on resource dependency and "objective" environmental forces, we will be ignorant of the ways in which relevant information is processed by decision makers and of social mechanisms that function to homogenize the perceptions of members. The dominant coalition in an organization is able to manipulate the situation in order to influence the manner in which the environment is perceived by members (Aldrich, 1979, pp. 157–159). If, on the other hand, we focus only upon information processing and responses to environment, we will ignore the influence that organizations have over their environment. Interaction between organizations and their environment does not occur on a one-way street. Organizations respond to environments, but we will see in Chapter 3 that organizations may also be capable of influencing their environments. Child (1972) uses the term "strategic choice" to refer to the discretion that an organization's dominant coalition has in responding to and even influencing its environment. In Chapter 3 we will look in detail at both proactive and reactive strategies available to enable organizations to "manage" their environments.

Benson (1975, p. 229) points out that systems are linked to a larger environment consisting of authorities, legislative bodies, publics, and bureaus. The flow of resources to a system depends upon changes and developments in the larger environment. For example, educational subsystems in communities are dependent upon municipal, state, and federal government for funding. Public universities are dependent upon state and federal government for funding and especially upon federal government for the funding of research. Warren (1967, pp. 414–418) states that deliberate changes in relationships between organizations in a system can be brought about by changes in funding patterns from outside the community, principally from various federal agencies. Subsystems within communities, like particular organizations within systems, compete for scarce resources. Competition for scarce dollars sets systems against each other within the community and within the larger society. Everyone is aware of the political battles over "guns or butter." Revenue sharing with its decentralized planning and decision making during the 1970s led to competition between organizations in many communities.

Emery and Trist (1965, pp. 24–26) have been concerned with trends in environmental conditions and have provided us with a useful typology of environments. Four ideal types of environment are described that can be ordered according to the degree of system connectedness existing among the components of the environment: placid and randomized, placid and clustered, disturbed-reactive, and turbulent. In the turbulent field, dynamic processes arise from the field itself and not merely from the interactions of components. According to Terreberry (1968), turbulent environments are complex, changing, and competitive, and the interactive effects of these characteristics may exceed the capacities of decision makers for prediction and hence control of the compounding consequences of their actions. Increasingly, environments for organizations are thought to be turbulent. This means that business executives, administrators in agencies, and political leaders will have to be flexible in their approach to the design of service delivery systems and take care to ensure that sufficient information for decision making is available.

SUMMARY

The reasons we need to understand more about IOR today fall into three categories: practical, ideological, and scientific. Lay persons readily recognize how relations between organizatons influence their lives. Social critics, persons concerned about community problems and the delivery of services, discuss these problems in terms of IOR. Business leaders sometimes find that joint ventures, and even corporate mergers, may be required in some situations.

Researchers have helped us realize that other organizations are among the most important elements in any organization's environment. Organizations that are interdependent influence each other, and if dependencies persist we can speak in terms of the emergence of community structure. An IOR model of the community may enable us to avoid geographical, romantic, and humanistic assumptions about communities.

The subsystem is the most basic unit of community analysis. Subsystems include particular organizations, dyads, and larger collectivities. Horizontal relations include linkages with other community units, and vertical relations include linkages with units at higher levels. Some think that the horizontal relations are weakening in many communities and vertical relations are growing stronger.

The specific environment of an organization includes the influences of other organizations in its input and output sets. Organizatons are also subject to the influences of general environmental factors. Environments are thought to be growing more turbulent, which means that obtaining information for decision making and obtaining required resources may be increasingly problematic.

DISCUSSION QUESTIONS

1. What are some of the reasons for understanding IOR in your community?
2. What are the geographic, romantic, and humanistic assumptions about communities?
3. What is the difference between a dyad and an organization set?
4. What is meant by an organization's specific environment?
5. Why are organizations interdependent?
6. Compare and contrast conceptions of the environment as information and as available resources.
7. What does the term "strategic choice" mean?

SUGGESTED ACTIVITIES

1. Discuss the organization sets of several organizations important to you.
2. Specify interstitial organizations that are of importance in your community.
3. Specify several kinds of horizontal and vertical linkages that are important for your community.

REFERENCES

Aldrich, H. E. Resource dependence and interorganizational relations. *Administration and Society*, 1976, 7, 419–453.

Aldrich, H. E. *Organizations and environments*. Englewood Cliffs, NJ: Prentice-Hall, 1979.

Aldrich, H. E., & Mindlin, S. Uncertainty and dependence: Two perspectives on environment. In L. Karpick (Ed.), *Organization and environment*. Beverly Hills, CA: Sage Publications, Inc., 1978, pp. 149–170.

Bates, F. L., & Bacon, L. The community as a social system. *Social Forces*, 1972, *53*, 371–379.

Benson, J. K. The interorganizational network as a political economy. *Administrative Science Quarterly*, 1975, *20*, 229–249.

Bernard, J. *The sociology of community*. Glenview, IL: Scott, Foresman, 1973.

Bertrand, A. L. *Social organization*. Philadelphia: F. A. Davis, 1972.

Blau, P. M., & Meyer, M. W. *Bureaucracy in modern society*. New York: Randon House, 1971.

Child, J. Organization structure, environment, and performance—The role of strategic choice. *Sociology*, 1972, *6*, 1–22.

Clark, B. R. Interorganizational patterns in education. *Administrative Science Quarterly*, 1965, *10*, 224–237.

Dill, W. R. Environment as an influence on managerial autonomy. *Administrative Science Quarterly*, 1958, *2*, 409–443.

Downey, H. K., & Ireland, R. D. Quantitative versus qualitative: Environmental assessment in organizational studies. *Administrative Science Quarterly*, 1979, *24*, 630–637.

Emery, F. E., & Trist, E. L. The causal texture of organizational environments. *Human Relations*, 1965, *18*, 21–32.

Evan, W. M. Toward a theory of inter-organizational relations. *Management Science*, 1965, *11*, 217–231.

Galaskiewicz, J. The structure of community organizational networks. *Social Forces*, 1979, *57*, 1346–1364.

Hall, R. H. *Organizations: Structure and process*. Englewood Cliffs, NJ: Prentice-Hall, 1977.

Katz, D., & Kahn, R. L. *The social psychology of organizations*. New York: John Wiley and Sons, 1978.

Marrett, C. B. On the specification of inter-organizational relations. *Sociology and Social Research*, 1971, *56*, 83–99.

Molnar, J. J., & Rogers, D. L. A comparative model of interorganizational conflict. *Administrative Science Quarterly*, 1979, *24*, 405–425.

Pfeffer, J., & Salancik, G. R. *The external control of organizations.* New York: Harper and Row, 1978.

Reid, W. Interagency coordination in delinquency prevention and control. *Social Service Review*, 1964, *38*, 418–427.

————Interorganizational coordination in social welfare: A theoretical approach to analysis and intervention. In R. M. Kramer & H. Specht (Eds.), *Readings in community organization practice.* Englewood Cliffs, NJ: Prentice-Hall, 1975, pp. 118–129.

Sanders, I. T. *The community: An introduction to a social system.* New York: The Ronald Press, 1966.

Terreberry, S. The evolution of organizational environments. *Administrative Science Quarterly*, 1968, *12*, 590–613.

Thompson, J. D. *Organizations in action.* New York: McGraw-Hill, 1967.

Turk, H. Interorganizational networks in urban society: Initial perspectives and comparative research. *American Sociological Review*, 1970, *35*, 1–19.

————Comparative urban structure from an interorganizational perspective. *Administrative Science Quarterly*, 1973, *18*, 37–55.

Warren, R. L. *The community in America.* Chicago: Rand McNally, 1963.

————The interorganizational field as a focus for investigation. *Administrative Science Quarterly*, 1967, *12*, 396–419.

————*Truth, love and social change.* Chicago: Rand McNally, 1971, pp. 129–224.

Young, R. C., & Larson, O. F. The contribution of voluntary organizations to community structure. *American Journal of Sociology*, 1965, *71*, 178–186.

Chapter 2

CONCEPTUALIZING INTERORGANIZATIONAL RELATIONS:

Units of Analysis and Key Dimensions

Until recently talking with automobile mechanics has always been unpleasant both for me and for them. We just hadn't been able to communicate. I would find myself describing a "strange noise somewhere up front" or something about the automobile's handling "that didn't feel right." The mechanics were always frustrated, too, because they didn't really know what my problem was. It finally occurred to me (perhaps it has for you too) that a minimum of technical knowledge and language is needed in order to communicate with these persons. I found and read a simple and straightforward book on automobile mechanics for consumers. Now when I talk to a mechanic, I describe the automobile system that is acting up and am more specific about what aspects of the system are presenting problems.

The possibility of not communicating well occurs every time we try to talk to any professional or expert. Being able to think in terms of significant units and using appropriate language to describe the ongoing operations is no less important when one begins to view the community from an interorganizational relations (IOR) perspective. In this chapter one goal is to become more familiar with the alternative units of analysis that can be used with the IOR perspective. We will see that the object of focus can vary from the IOR of particular organizations to the collectivities including whole community subsystems, depending upon the kinds of questions we are asking about the community. Another goal is to become familiar with the range of relationships (linkage mechanisms) that can be found and with the dimensions used to describe them. In a sense we will be creating an IOR map of the community comparable to a blueprint or schematic design of a mechanical system. This map of the "IOR terrain" will allow us to view the community as a system of systems with both horizontal and vertical linkages. In the chapters that immediately follow, models that explain the development and consequences of IOR will be presented and evaluated.

UNITS OF ANALYSIS

Taking his departure from the utility of the concept of role set developed by Merton (1957, pp. 368–380) for analyzing role relations, Evan (1965, pp. 218–226) has stated that each focal organization's immediate environment consists of an organization set. This set can be further broken down into input and output components. A focal organization depends upon input organizations for resources and produces a product, performs a service, etc., that it distributes to or through other organizations. A focal organization can have a relatively small or large number of organizations in its set.

Evan has discussed the focal organization's autonomy in decision making and has developed propositions that relate to dimensions of organization sets. For example, Evan has hypothesized that if resources are concentrated in only a few organizations or an uncooperative coalition formation develops, the focal organization's autonomy will be limited. Evan hypothesizes that similarity of functions between the focal organization and the members of its set will lead to competition but complementarity of functions will lead to cooperation. In addition, if the members of an organization set exhibit a high rate of technical change, the focal organizaton will, in order to remain competitive, be highly receptive to innovations.

Thompson (1962) has alerted us to the importance of transaction structures between the focal organization and the members in its set. Organizations have input and output roles designed to arrange the acquisition of resources and distribution of the organization's services, products, or impact to others. Input and output roles are boundary-spanning roles linking organizations and environment through interaction between member and nonmember. Each output and input role, together with its reciprocating nonmember role, can be seen as a transaction structure. Thompson has provided us with a framework for analyzing transaction structures and their outcomes and has developed a typology of transaction structures. The typology is based upon two dimensions; the extent to which the organization's agents are controlled and programmed and the extent to which nonmembers are compelled to participate in the relationship. A clerk interacting with a customer in a supermarket illustates the programmed-optional structure. A social worker interacting with a client in a private agency illustrates the nonprogrammed-optional structure. Organizations faced with transaction structures in which the nonmembers are not compelled to interact will attempt to limit the freedom and options of nonmembers; achievement of a monopoly does this immediately. Actually, many government agencies and public schools are monopolistic. Can you think of other examples of monopolies in your community?

For any transaction structure there are three possible outcomes: completion of the transaction, abortion, or a side transaction. Thompson proposes that the most likely paths from initiation to termination and the branching points that lead to one or another outcome are largely determined by the type of transaction structure. Thompson's ideas about transaction structures should add to our understanding of relationships between a focal organization and the organizations in its set.

Interorganizational collectivities (ICs) (Van de Ven et al., 1975) include two or more organizations, with the simplest collectivity being the dyad. A subsystem of the community, such as the education subsystem, would include all of the smaller collectivities. Organizations in a collectivity may work together to perform a series of goal-directed behavioral acts. For example, two organizations may develop a joint activity for youth, or two businesses may develop a joint business venture. A hypothetical illustration portraying focal organizations, sets, and collectivities is presented in Figure 2-1.

Six ICs, plus the overall collectivity, are shown in Figure 2-1. The group shelter home and county probation are crucial organizations because they link the other organizations together. Linkages to organizations in other systems promote community integration. Note that an organization set is not the same as a collectivity. According to Evan's (1965) definition of an organization set, if group shelter home (01) is the focal organization for our analysis, organizations 02, 03, 04, 05, 06, and 07 are included in its set. Probation (03) has organizations 01, 02, 05, and 08 in its set. The mental health center (06) has only two organizations in its set and the employment agency and the churches have only the group shelter home in their sets. The group shelter home is a member of five collectivities plus the overall collectivity, and its motivation for membership in each may be different.

Van de Ven and his colleagues (1975, pp. 27–30) very correctly point out that ICs, like organizations, are not distinguished by their membership but by their functional goals, role structure, and behavior as a system. Further, two or more ICs composed of the same member organizations may exist in a given environment at the same point in time. For example, it is noted that retail business organizations, by the nature of their trade and a limited sales market, may be forced together into a cutthroat competitive IC, and at the same time may be joined in a cooperative IC sponsored by the chamber of commerce. The most comprehensive units of analysis are the subsystems, including the economic, religious, educational, governmental, health-welfare, leisure, and family subsystems, which are themselves composed of smaller collectivities (Sanders, 1966; Warren, 1963).

In Chapter 1 we learned that Hall (1977, pp. 303–332) has provided a framework for analyzing the general and specific en-

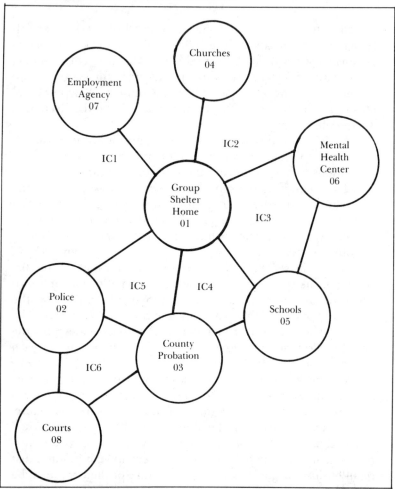

Figure 2-1. A Hypothetical Network of Organizations That Serve Problem Youth.

vironments of particular organizations, collectivities, and subsystems. The specific environment includes those organizations with which particular organizations or ICs interact. Interaction also occurs between subsystems, and the relative power and dependency of particular subsystems can be evaluated.

Increasingly, the importance of vertical linkages to more

comprehensive systems at state and federal levels are being noted. Warren (1978, pp. 423–436) points out that a large part of what takes place locally cannot be adequately understood without considering this important vertical dimension: local communities cannot be seen as closed systems or islands unto themselves. Warren suggests that we might consider communities as local enactments of the macrosystem, as the nodes of implementation of the national society. This approach suggested by Warren does, however, require further systematic analysis and more adequate conceptualization of the interface between aspects of the macrosystem and local community. In particular, a more precise specification of the nature of the linkages between subsystems at the local level and systems at a higher level is required.

The adoption of Warren's perspective will drastically alter our understanding of community development and intervention. It should be noted that some "community problems" such as unemployment and lack of funding for education, may not really be solvable by local communities. Some community development activities may have to be directed at higher vertical levels, for that is where the local community's fate may be primarily determined. This doesn't mean, however, that horizontal ties with other local units, or with units in nearby communities are unimportant. If inflation and competition for funds continue, state and federal agencies will be able to provide fewer services for local persons. The solution of many problems and the provision of many services will require that local communities provide the needed resources or that stronger horizontal ties within and between communities be developed to facilitate the delivery of services.

The information presented to this point is summarized in Figure 2-2. Examples of focal organizations, linkages, sets, dyads, and larger collectivities are presented for three institutions found in communities. Note, again, that an advantage of the IOR perspective is that your unit of analysis (level or abstraction) can range from a macrofocus upon whole subsystems, to smaller collectivities, to an analysis of the IOR for particular organizations. The correct, or apropriate, unit of analysis depends entirely upon the question at hand, with different kinds of questions being answered by different levels of analysis.

Figure 2-2. Examples of Units of Analysis for Interorganizational Perspective.

	Institutions		
	Economic	*Government*	*Education*
Interorgani-zational Collectivity	Employment agency; business organizations, such as Chamber of Commerce and Kiwanis; Industrial Development Corporation; and local business seeking new businesses.	Mayor's office, city manager's office, city council and various local services preparing a five-year plan.	Board of education, schools, professional organizations, and citizen advisory organizations doing a needs assessment study.
Dyad	Employment agency working with a specific local grocery store.	Interaction between city manager's office and police department.	Two junior high schools sharing the cost of hiring a band director.
Set	Includes the wholesale firms that provide grocery items, firms that provide services and	Includes the city council, mayor's office and local services such as police and fire that interact with	Includes the local schools and advisory groups that interact with local board of education.

(Continued)

	maintenance, and organizations that buy products from a particular grocery store.	city manager's office.	
Vertical Linkage	Interaction between local grocery stores and regional office with regard to sales trends.	Federal agency awarding grant to local police department for purchase of needed equipment.	State department of education's certification of high school curriculum.
Focal Organization	"XYZ Grocery."	The local police department.	Senior high school.

In summary, when particular organizations are studied, our attention is focused upon input and output activities. In addition, the impact of IOR on organizational structure and functioning can be determined. The influence of organization-set size and diversity can be determined. When dyads, or larger collectivities are studied, the focus is upon interaction between organizations. Warren (1967, pp. 402–403) refers to the overall pattern or network of relations as the "field," and points out that the interaction between any two particular organizations is affected in part by the field itself. A complete network, if each organization has relations with each of the others, will contain $\frac{n(n-1)}{2}$ pairwise relationships, where n is the number of organizations. When larger collectivities and whole networks are the subject of our interest, our primary focus shifts from the relationship between pairs of organizations to patterns of relationships among the collectivity of organizations bound together by allied domains, an interest in common client populations, or shared problems (Levine and White, 1961, pp. 597).

STRUCTURAL DIMENSIONS AND INTENSITY OF IOR

We are most interested in the stable and typical patterns of interaction that exist between organizations and collectivities because these patterns of IOR, be they cooperative and/or based upon conflict, have the greatest influence. The term "social structure," as used here, denotes patterns of IOR. Some of the key dimensions stressed and most relevant questions and issues raised in an analysis of IOR are presented in Figure 2-3.

The predominant approach to examining the structure of IOR has been to identify nominal classifications of relationships, such as mediated, where a third party influences the relationship between the organizations versus *ad hoc* or unmediated relationships (Reid, 1964). Bates (1974, pp. 4–5) has distinguished between "invisible-hand" influences and "visible-hand" influences on IOR. Examples of the invisible hand operating would be when the government regulates the conditions under which business organizations relate to each other. In such situations legislative bodies constitute forums in which conflicting interests can seek advantage under conditions of controlled conflict. The judicial system operates to provide a means of settling disputes. Visible-hand control means that the interacting organizations are subject to a common authority structure that has the responsibility for coordinating the operations of the system. Visible-hand relationships can be seen operating in agencies of government and within business corporations.

Clark (1965) has discussed federated versus corporate structures of IOR, and Warren (1967, p. 404) has pointed out the distinctions between unitary, federative, coalitional, and social choice configurations of IOR. These configurations can be distinguished from each other in terms of the relations of member

Figure 2-3. Units of Analysis, Dimensions Stressed, and Examples of Relevant Issues and Questions.

	Units of Analysis					
	IOR of Particular Organizations	Dyadic Relations			Larger Collectivities	
			Relational Properties			
	Characteristics of Organizations	Comparative Properties	Dimensions	Linkage Mechanisms	Formal Contextual Properties	General Environmental Dimensions
Dimensions Stressed	e.g., size, innovativeness, complexity, openness, and autonomy.	e.g., homogeneity of structure and function, awareness of other parties, stability, size and philosophies.	e.g., intensity, reciprocity, standardization, and formality.	e.g., modes of coordination, administrative and direct service linkage mechanisms.	e.g., network size, extra-local and local integration, and history of interlocking relations.	e.g., munificence, interconnectedness, and concentration.
Relevant Issues and Questions	1. Frequency of IOR. 2. Kinds of IOR. 3. Impact of IOR on organizational structure and processes.		1. "With whom" do organizations interact? 2. What linkages develop most often? 3. What properties are associated most frequently with linkages?		1. What contextual properties lead to new IOR? 2. How are contextual properties changing? 3. How do properties of IOR systems influence specific organizations? 4. What is the impact of whole networks and community-wide structures?	

organizations to an inclusive goal, locus of decision making, provision for division of labor, commitment to a leadership subsystem, and presence or absence of a collectivity orientation of member organizations. Nominal classifications of IOR relationships such as these, however, serve only limited purposes for us. In contrast to nominal classifications, an approach that emphasizes a dimensional method of defining and studying structure has several advantages. The dimensional method is more inclusive and general. Utilizing appropriate dimensions, the analyst can consider the whole array of alternative kinds of IOR structure, which will provide greater potential for drawing inferences from one situation to another (Van de Ven, 1980, p. 303).

Distinct approaches to specifying relevant IOR dimensions are reflected in the literature (Marrett, 1971). The approaches vary according to the unit of analysis emphasized, e.g., particular organizations, dyads, or large collectivities (see Figure 2-3). The dominant approach used has been to focus on intraorganizational properties of organizations. Studies in this vein have analyzed particular organizations' characteristics affecting or affected by their interaction with other organizations.

Researchers have sought to identify the frequency and kinds of IOR developed by particular organizations. In her review of the literature, Marrett (1971, pp. 85–86) points out that it is generally thought that complex organizations that are more innovative, have more openness of communication, are autonomous from parent bodies, lack access to outside resources, and have favorable roles or norms are more likely to interact with other organizations. When our attention is focused upon particular organizations, no analysis of the specific interaction with other organizations itself is required. For example, in one of the most widely quoted studies, Aiken and Hage (1968) have established that complex health and social welfare organizations are more likely to be innovative in their program development, and these organizations are more likely to establish joint programs with other organizations to help pay for the costs of the added innovations. In their analysis, the major dependent variable was the number of joint programs, but no analysis was made of the specific joint programs or their effectiveness.

Studies formally classified as interorganizational focus upon the interaction occurring between organizations. Dyads are actually the simplest unit of IOR. Because they are the simplest IOR units, interest in dyads has increased greatly. Specialists interested in dyadic relations examine appropriate comparative and relational properties. Paulson (1976) has correctly pointed out that organizational properties may be a clue as to which organizations are most likely to interact, but not "with whom." "With whom" concerns can only be answered by considering comparative properties such as size, scarcity of resources, and goals and functions.

The comparative-properties approach has been concerned with identifying and understanding how relevant comparative properties can lead to cooperation and/or conflict. Comparative properties thought to be important include homogeneity (in terms of structure and function), awareness of other parties, stability, resources available and needed, number of resource sources, overlap in membership, size, compatibility of philosophies, social status, and professionalism. In addition to these comparative properties, concern has also been shown for relative legitimacy or domain consensus, e.g., the degree to which organizations' goals are disputed, seen to overlap, or are seen as incompatible (Marrett, 1971; Mulford, 1981; Paulson, 1976; Van de Ven et al, 1975) with other organizations' goals.

Two approaches predominate for examining relational properties between organizations. One emphasizes the dimensions of interaction between organizations while the second approach emphasizes mechanisms for establishing and maintaining linkages between organizations (Van de Ven et al., 1975, pp. 24–26).

Marrett (1971) has led the way in pointing out the importance of understanding the dimensions (characteristics) of interaction that occur in dyads and larger collectivities. Our discussion here relies heavily upon her analysis. The degree of formality is an importent dimension because formal agreements between organizations may be relatively hard to terminate if they are not satisfactory; and because formal agreements reduce autonomy, organizations may be reluctant to enter into them. A second aspect of formality has to do with the extent to which an intermediary organization coordinates the relationship involving other organizations. Relations also differ in terms of another characteristic, intensity. Two dimensions of intensity are relevant: the size of the resource investment involved and the frequency of interaction. Unless the organizations have slack resources to use or have worked well with each other in the past, there may be reluctance to choose intense involvement.

Reciprocity has to do with the direction in which resources flow. With symmetrical relations, both organizations benefit, but only one benefits in asymmetrical exchange. Mutual dependence, which means that each organization in the dyad needs the other, can be contrasted with asymmetric dependence. Organizations may be reluctant to participate in unbalanced relationships. Related to formalization, standardization has to do with the degree to which fixed units of exchange exist, and the degree to which fixed procedures for exchange exist. It should be noted that even if formal agreements exist between organizations, if a flexible working arrangement is desired, set rules and procedures may be at a minimum. Standardization is more likely when formal agreements do exist.

Marrett proposes that two models of relationships (ideal types) can be conceptualized. With the first model, dyadic relations are characterized by a low degree of formality, standardization, and intensity. Reciprocity may not be a crucial consideration with this model. This model would be represented by the kinds of interaction that frequently occur between health and social welfare organizations, with reference to client referrals. In the second model, dyadic relations are characterized by relatively high degrees of formality, standardization, and intensity. Reciprocity will more than likely be a relevant concern because the organizations' autonomy is affected and investments the organizations may not be willing to make are involved.

Alternative modes of coordination for the delivery of human services have been described, including voluntary, mediated, and directed coordination (Aiken et al., 1975; Gans and Horton, 1975). Gans and Horton (pp. 11–14, 37–39, 91–93) have specified a wide variety of kinds of linkages (the mechanisms for maintaining coordination), the effort required to develop the linkages, and their relative impact. Two categories of linkages are described: administrative and direct service. Administrative linkage mechanisms include fiscal linkages such as joint budgeting, joint funding, colocation of staff, and administrative support services. Direct service linkages include referrals and case coordination.

Another approach seen in the literature stresses the larger context in which IOR occur and the overall structure and processes that occur within larger collectivities. Studies (Marrett, 1971, pp. 87–88) that emphasize a formal contextual approach explore the influences of existing overall system properties in IOR. Prominent examples in the literature emphasize the importance of formal, contextual properties, e.g., degree of extralocal and local integration (Turk, 1970), the size of the existing organizational set (Evan, 1965), and the previous history of interlocking relations (Aiken and Alford, 1970). The work of Turk is especially innnovative in that he has been studying the emergence of new IOR in 130 large American cities. A clear concern for the influence of general environmental factors is also present in the literature. Clark (1965), for example, has discussed the impact of political, economic, and demographic changes on educational systems. Warren (1967) has called our attention to the larger "field" within which IOR occur and suggests that environmental elements may exert significant influence on the persistence and expansion of IOR.

Pfeffer and Salancik (1978, pp. 62–70) conclude, after their own review of the literature, that the three most elemental structural characteristics of environments are concentration, munificence, and interconnectedness. Concentration has to do with the extent to which power and authority are dispersed, and munificence involves the extent to which resources are available. Interconnectedness, a dimension receiving more and more attention, has to do with the number and pattern of linkages, or connections, among organizations. Interconnectedness is clearly illustrated by the far-ranging economic, military, and social impacts that have resulted from the greatly increased cost of energy. Pfeffer and Salancik conclude, too, that interconnectedness is increasing and that the cause is most often government action.

These three dimensions are important because they in turn are thought to determine the relationships among organizations— for example, the degree of conflict and interdependence present. Conflict and interdependence are thought to determine, at least in part, the uncertainty that organizations confront. For other discussions of environmental characteristics, see Aldrich (1979) and Child (1972).

CUMULATIVE INTENSITY OF IOR

Past studies have largely ignored the cumulative nature of IOR involvement. It has been assumed that less intense linkages, such as information exchanges, usually have to precede resouce exchanges and formal agreements because the latter are more costly and require greater commitment. Aiken and Hage (1968) used a single item (the number of joint programs) in their research to measure high-level involvement. Levine and White (1961) used a series of IOR measures but developed no composite measure. Paulson (1974) used two items (number of joint programs and resource exchanges) but did not develop a composite measure or investigate their cumulative effect. A cumulative scale of IOR would be helpful because it would specify the sequential stages through which organizations move as they interact with each other. A cumulative scale, if one can be developed, would have both theoretical and practical implications. For example, we would be able to analyze the comparative properties that lead to more intense and cumulative IOR. From an applied and action point of view, we would be able to think about the barriers and facilitators of increasingly intense IOR, and we would be able to provide more insights into the planning needed when moving from one stage to another.

Rogers' (1974) article, one of the first published descriptions of an effort to develop a cumulative scale of intensity, acknowledges the previous but unpublished work of others (Finley, 1969; Klonglan et al., 1972). Rogers did find some evidence to support the notion of a sequential scale. Specificially, Rogers found that the stages of IOR proceeded from director acquaintance to director interaction, information exchange, resource exchange, overlapping boards, and finally written agreement. Evidence presented by Rogers suggested that the scale was a reliable and valid instrument for describing the IOR between the county level offices of 10 public agencies.

Since Rogers' (1974) published scale did not include all eight of the items previously developed (Klonglan et al., 1972), one goal of the research completed later by Klonglan and his colleagues (1976) was to analyze the merits of a cumulative scale containing all eight steps. Secondly, an important goal was to determine if the stages of IOR occurred in the same sequential pattern for three distinct hierarchical levels: for interaction between organizations at the county level, multicounty district level, and state level.

The eight items used by Klonglan et al. (1976) and their rationale are presented below.

Suggested Scale Items	*Source and Relevancy*
1. *Director Awareness:* As far as you know, is there (name of other organization) in this (state, area, or county)?	Litwak and Hylton (1962), awareness of independence.
2. *Director Acquaintance:* Are you acquainted with the director or person in charge of (contact organization)?	Litwak and Hylton (1962), awareness of independence.
3. *Director Interaction:* Have you met with the director of (contact organization) at any time during the past year to discuss the activities of your respective organizations?	Litwak and Hylton (1962), awareness of independence.
4. *Information Exchange:* Is your organization on (contact organization's) mailing list to receive newsletters, annual reports, or other	Finley (1969), low level of resource exchange.

Suggested *Scale Items*	*Source and* *Relevancy*

information? Or: Is (contact organization) on your organization's mailing list to receive any of your newsletters, annual reports, or other information releases?

5. *Resource Exchange:* Has your organization shared, loaned, or provided resources such as meeting rooms, personnel, equipment, or funds to (contact organization) at any time during the last three years? Or: Has (contact organization) shared, loaned, or provided resources such as meeting rooms, personnel, equipment, or funds to your organization at any time during the last three years?

Thompson and McEwen (1958), resource exchange—bargaining.

6. *Overlapping Boards or Councils:* Does anyone from your organization or (contact organization) including staff, board members, or members serve on boards, councils or committees of the other organizations?

Thompson and McEwen (1958), overlapping board membership—cooptation.

7. *Joint Programs:* Within the last three years, has your organization worked jointly in planning and implementing any specific programs or activities with (contact organization)?

Thompson and McEwen (1958), joint programs—coalition.

Suggested Scale Items	*Source and Relevancy*
8. *Written Agreements:* Does your organization have any written agreements with (contact organization) pertaining to personnel commitments, client referrals, procedures for working together, or other joint activities?	Litwak and Hylton (1962), standardization

The first item or form of IOR specifies that the director of the organization in question is only aware of the existence of another organization. The next two forms represent low-level and preliminary interaction. If the level of IOR is not sufficient, organizations may proceed to higher levels of intensity. Joint programs and written agreements are relatively more costly and threatening forms of IOR and only occur after other forms have occurred according to the proposed scale. Parenthetically, it should be noted that Rogers (1974) did not use items 1 or 7 in his scale analysis efforts.

Do IOR occur in sequential stages as suggested? The published results are helpful but not as strong and consistent as we would hope. Overall, empirical results follow the suggested sequential ordering to a significant degree only for organizations that interact at the district level. Across the three hierarchical levels, five of the eight forms of interaction occur in the same order as shown below.

Scale Items Consistent Across Three Levels	*Original Item Number*
1. Director Awareness	1st
2. Director Acquaintance	2nd
3. Director Interaction	3rd
4. Overlapping Boards	6th
5. Written Agreements	8th

Most of the inconsistency involved original items 4, 5, and 6. Information exchanges, resource exchanges, and overlapping boards did not always occur in the expected order, or even in the same actual order for the three hierarchical levels. The three items that changed order may be clues to the qualitative distinction between the levels. The state level organizations in this study depend upon information exchange (third) much more than upon joint programs (fifth), or resource exchange (sixth). County level organizations depend upon resource exchange (third) more than information exchange (fifth), or joint programs (sixth). The district level organizations depend upon joint programs (third) more than information exchange (fifth) or resource exchange (sixth).

The distinct feature of district IOR is the inclusion of the relatively enduring form of joint programs. Why does this occur? It could be due to the nature of the unique social services sector organizations studied. Or it could mean that the setting (the environment) for district level organizations is such that joint programs can be developed without prior director interaction, information exchange, or resource exchanges. Perhaps there is less turnover of personnel at district level offices or there are fewer district level offices than those found at state or local levels, which would mean that director acquaintances and information exchanges are not as crucial. District level offices may have fewer resource needs of the kind specified in the scale that can be satisfied by other district level offices.

The results reported by Klonglan, et al.(1976) clearly point out the need to consider the important distinctions between county, district office, and state level IOR. In terms of the search for a cumulative scale that can be used in all situations, that goal has not been reached (unless you are content to use the five items that are consistent across all hierarchical levels studied). Obviously, a cumulative scale would be very helpful, but much work remains to be done in its development.

SUMMARY

It is necessary to become familiar with the alternative units of analysis and key dimensions that describe relationships between organizations in order to appreciate the full range of questions and issues that can be analayzed with an IOR perspective. Each focal organization's immediate environment consists of an organization set. Information and resources are obtained from input organizations and services and products are provided for other organizations by the focal organization. The characteristics of an organization set can act as constraints and influence the behavior of an organization.

Interorganizational collectivities include dyads and more comprehensive units. Subsystems of the community include all of the smaller units. It has been stated that vertical linkages connecting local organizations with those at higher levels are increasing in importance. While the importance of some vertical linkages may be increasing, the resolution of some community problems still requires horizontal linkages between local organizations and perhaps linkages between organizations from different communities.

Studies of particular organizations and their IOR have predominated until recently. Persons have been concerned about the frequency with which particular organizations establish relationships with others and with the impact of these relationships on the organizations. Comparative organizational properties such as comparative structures, size, and philosophies held by members are thought to determine the likelihood of relationships between particular pairs of organizations. When larger and more comprehensive collectivities have been the focus of interest, efforts have been made to determine the influence of contextual properties and environmental dimensions on the emergence and persistence of networks.

There is some evidence to suggest that the interaction between organizations proceeds along a sequential and cumulative scale. These results mean that it may be difficult to get organizations that have not worked together before to participate in joint ventures involving significant organizational resources.

Now that we have become familiar with the "IOR terrain" and the perspective required for understanding the terrain, we are prepared to begin our analysis in earnest. In Chapter 3 we will learn why particular organizations develop relationships with others and how they are affected by these relationships.

DISCUSSION QUESTIONS

1. What is the difference between an organization set and a collectivity? Give an example of each.

2. Compare and contrast any two different transaction structures in your community.

3. How do you think comparative properties can influence relationships between organizations? What are some of the most relevant comparative properties?

4. What determines whether formal, intense, reciprocal, and standardized relationships between organizations are best, or if other kinds of relationships are best?

SUGGESTED ACTIVITIES

1. Think about two or three organizations in your community. Can you identify several of their vertical and horizontal linkages?

2. Discuss some "community problem" that may be solvable only through the strengthening of vertical IOR.

3. What evidence can you cite to support the notion that horizontal ties, relative to vertical ones, are becoming weaker in your community?

4. Can you give examples to illustrate how the environmental characteristics discussed (concentration, munificence and interconnectedness) are affecting organizations in your community?

REFERENCES

Aiken, M., & Hage, J. Organizational interdependence and intraorganizatonal structure. *American Sociological Review*, 1968, *33*, 912–930.

Aiken, M., & Alford, R. Community structure and innovation. *American Sociological Review*, 1970, *35*, 650–665.

Aiken, M., Dewar, R., Di Tomaso, N., Hage, J., & Zeitz, G. *Coordinating human services*. San Francisco: Jossey-Bass, 1975.

Aldrich, H. E. *Organizations and environments*. Englewood Cliffs, NJ: Prentice-Hall, 1979.

Bates, F. L. Alternative models for the future of society: From the invisible hand to the visible hand. *Social Forces*, 1974, *53*, 1–11.

Child, J. Organizational structure, environment and performance: The role of strategic choice. *Sociology*, 1972, *6*, 1–22.

Clark, B. R. Interorganizational patterns in education. *Administrative Science Quarterly*, 1965, *10*, 327–336.

Evan, W. M. Toward a theory of interorganizational relations. *Management Science*, 1965, *11*, 217–231.

Finley, J. R. Relations between development organizations: A preliminary report of scaling interorganizational relations. Paper presented at the Rural Sociological Society Meetings, San Francisco, CA, 1969.

Gans, S. P., & Horton, G. T. *Integration of human services*. New York: Praeger, 1975.

Hall, R. H. *Organizations: Structure and process*. Englewood Cliffs, NJ: Prentice-Hall, 1972.

Klonglan, G. E., Paulson, S. K., & Rogers, D. L. Measurement of interorganizational relations: A deterministic model. Paper presented at the American Sociological Association Meeting, New Orleans, LA, 1972.

Klonglan, G. E., Warren, R. D., Winkelpleck, J. M., & Paulson, S. K. Interorganizational measurement in the social service sector: Differences by hierarchical level. *Administrative Science Quarterly*, 1976, *21*, 675–687.

Levine, S., & White, P. E. Exchange as a conceptual framework for the study of interorganizational relationships. *Administrative Science Quarterly*, 1961, *5*, 583–610.

Litwak, E., & Hylton, L. Interorganizational analysis: A hypothesis on coordinating agencies. *Administrative Science Quarterly*, 1962, *7*, 395–420.

Marrett, C. B. On the specification of interorganizational relations. *Sociology and Social Research*, 1971, *56*, 83–99.

Merton, R. K. *Social theory and social structure*. Glencoe, IL: The Free Press, 1957.

Mulford, C. L., & Zober, E. S. Dyadic properties as correlates of exchange and conflict between organizations. Paper presented at the Midwest Sociological Society Meetings, Minneapolis, MN, 1981.

Paulson, S. K. Causal analysis of interorganizational relations: an axiomatic theory revised. *Administrative Science Quarterly*, 1974, *19*, 319–337.

———A theory and comparative analysis of interorganizational dyads. *Rural Sociology*, 1976, *41*, 311–329.

Pfeffer, J., & Salancik, G. R. *The External control of organizations*. New York: Harper and Row, 1978.

Reid, W. Interagency coordination in delinquency prevention and control. *Social Service Review*, 1964, *38*, 418–427.

Rogers, D. L. Towards a scale of interorganizational relations among public agencies. *Sociology and Social Research*, 1974, *59*, 61–70.

Sanders, I. T. *The community: An introduction to a social system*. New York: The Ronald Press, 1966.

Thompson, J. D., & McEwen, W. J. Organizational goals and environment: Goal-setting as an interaction process. *American Sociological Review*, 1958, *23*, 23–31.

Thompson, J. D. Organizations and output transactions. *American Journal of Sociology*, 1962, *68*, 309–324.

Turk, H. Interorganizational networks in urban society: Initial perspectives and comparative research. *American Sociological Review*, 1970, *35*, 1–19.

Van de Ven, A. H. *Measuring and assessing organizations*. New York: John Wiley and Sons, 1980.

Van de Ven, A. H., Emmett, D. R., & Koening, R. Jr. Frameworks for interorganizational analysis. In A. R. Neghandi (Ed.), *Interorganizational theory*. Kent, OH: Kent State University Press, 1975, pp. 19–48.

Warren, R. L. *The community in America.* Chicago: Rand McNally, 1963.

————The interorganizational field as a focus for investigation. *Administrative Science Quarterly,* 1967, *12,* 398–419.

————*The community in America.* Chicago: Rand McNally, 1978.

Chapter 3

THE EXTERNAL RELATIONS OF PARTICULAR ORGANIZATIONS:

Strategies for Managing Environments

This chapter focuses upon the causes and consequences of interaction between particular organizations and their environments. As a way of recalling the importance of interaction between organizations and their environments, think for a minute about the worst organization that you have ever encountered and then about the best organization that you have ever encountered. What was it about these particular organizations and the relationships with their environments that made them so bad or so good? Were resources readily available for their use? Were there available markets for their products or services? Did strong competition threaten the ineffective organizations? Did the organizations become blind to changes occurring in their environments and to the needs of their clientele? These are some of the reasons for ineffectiveness mentioned by people.

The point is that people are almost never able to discuss effective organizations without mentioning their environments! Lay persons readily understand that much can be gained by viewing organizations as semiopen systems that interact with their environments rather than as closed systems that exist as islands unto themselves.

In this chapter our attention is directed toward three objectives. First, we will discuss the conceptualization of organization-environment relations and the dominant models of organization-environment interaction. Secondly, organizational "strategies" for managing environments will be evaluated. Our third objective will be to review some of the ways in which organizational structure and necessary functioning for effectiveness are thought to be contingent upon environments. Finally, we will analyze the results of empirical studies done of organizatons attempting to manage their environments and the results of studies completed in order to evaluate contingency hypotheses.

ENVIRONMENTS OF ORGANIZATIONS

Consistent with Thompson (1967, pp. 6–9) and Aldrich (1979, pp. 4–6), organizations can be seen as goal-directed, semiopen activity systems. This definition places an emphasis on task-oriented behavior that occurs as the activities of participants are directed toward some common purpose. The focus on activity systems alerts us to the ongoing processes in organizations influenced by the technology utilized. Organizations must be able to control their own boundaries in order to maintain their autonomy, but autonomy is a matter of degree for nearly all organizations because they are semiopen. Organizational needs include members, resources, information, and markets. Organizations are not completely open, however, or their boundaries would cease and no autonomy would be possible.

Power in organizations is sought by coalitions with varying and sometimes incompatible interests and is thought to be related to the possession of critical and scarce resources. Coalition formation (Pennings and Goodman, 1977) permits an organization to function in spite of varying and incompatible interests. The dominant coalition, representing a combination of constituencies, chooses goals for the organization and chooses the means for attaining these goals. Pfeffer and Salancik (1978, pp. 2–14, 228–244) note that organizations survive to the extent to which they are effective. Effectiveness derives from the management and

fulfillment of demands of interest groups upon which the organization is dependent for resources and support. Effectiveness,
then, is sociopolitical and is determined largely by external
standards. Efficiency, on the other hand, has to do with the ratio
of resources used over output and is largely an internal concern
of management.

Thompson (1967, pp. 13–56) was among the first to state
that the central problem facing organizations is uncertainty, with
existing technologies and environments being the major sources.
The dominant coalition uses an appropriate configuration of coordination strategies to eliminate uncertainty caused by interdependent technologies within the organization. Pooled interdependencies, in which each unit renders a discrete contribution,
are best coordinated through standardization, the development
of rules to promote unified action. Sequential interdependence
refers to situations where the outputs from some units serve as
inputs for other units and planning is required in which the
schedule of activities for the units takes place. With reciprocal
interdependence, the outputs of each unit are the inputs for
others, and coordination through mutual adjustment is appropriate.

Technical rationality is achieved when an organization succeeds in producing the desired goods, services, or products with
the least necessary expenditure of resources. Thompson has also
discussed a larger sense of "configuration" which he called "coalignment." The co-alignment of organizational technology, input
and output requirements, realities of the environment, and appropriate organizational structure is the most basic administrative
function. Technical rationality alone, Thompson cautioned, is a
necessary component but not sufficient by itself to provide "organizational rationality," which requires that the technology, environmental consideration, and organization structure be appropriately geared to each other (pp. 146–147).

Environmental Dimensions

Environmental contingencies for particular organizations
originate from the general environment and from specific environmental influences on the organization. General environ-

mental conditions include technological conditions and developments and legal, political, economic, demographic, ecological, and cultural conditions (Hall, 1977, pp. 304–312). Child (1972, pp. 3–5), Aldrich (1979, pp. 63–74), and Pfeffer and Salancik (1978, pp. 63–70), who have reviewed the extensive literature on environments, have specified the following key dimensions to describe environments.

Aldrich

1. *Concentration-Dispersion:* the degree resources are evenly distributed.
2. *Environmental Capability:* relative level of resources available.
3. *Homogeneity-Heterogeneity:* degree of similarity between individuals and organizations.
4. *Domain Consensus:* degree that organizations' claims to domains are disputed or recognized.
5. *Stability-Instability:* degree of turnover in environmental elements.
6. *Turbulence:* extent environment is characterized by increasing interconnection between elements and rate of interconnection.

Pfeffer and Salancik

1. *Concentration:* entent to which power and authority in the environment is widely dispersed.
2. *Munificence:* the availability or scarcity of resources.
3. *Interconnectedness:* the number and pattern of linkages.

Child

1. *Change:* frequency of changes in environmental activities, differences involved at each change, and irregularity in pattern of change.

2. *Complexity:* degree of heterogeneity and range of activities relevant to an organization's activities.

3. *Illiberality:* degree of threat resulting from competition, hostility, or even indifference.

The three sets of dimensions are really more comparable than they are different. To the degree that these conditions exist, organizations will find their behavior constrained. In particular, organization decision makers will have to take actions to guarantee a supply of resources and in order to obtain information needed for decision making. While these environmental conditions, if present, influence all organizations to some degree, specific environmental influences originate in the task environments of organizations.

The Task Environment of Organizations

Hall's (1977, p. 304) concept of "specific environment" is a slight modification of Thompson's (1967) notion of "task environment" and of Dill's (1958) notion of "relevant environment" which refers to those elements in the environment that are actually, or potentially, relevant for an organization. Other organizations are very important elements in a particular organization's specific environment. To achieve their goals, organizations must, in varying degrees, depend upon the environment for a variety of resources such as personnel, information, monetary and physical resources, clients, customers or markets (Aiken and Hage, 1968; Levine and White, 1961; Thompson, 1967). Resources are obtained from organizations in the particular focal organization's input set. The convention we will follow here is to use the term "focal organization" when referring to a particular organization in relation to its organization set. The focal organization's products, services, or other contributions are frequently channeled through, or evaluated by, organizations in its output set (Evan, 1965).

Evan (1965, pp. 220–224) has suggested that an analysis of the organizations in the set of a focal organization can help explain many things, including the focal organization's

1. internal structure,
2. degree of autonomy,
3. degree of goal attainment,
4. public image,
5. flow of information to the focal organization and to the set members,
6. flow of personnel, and
7. forces impelling the focal organization to cooperate with organizations in its set, or coordinate with members, to merge with other organizations, or to discontinue relationships.

For example, it has been suggested that when resources are concentrated and under the control of a few organizations in the set, a focal organization's autonomy will be lessened. In addition, it has been proposed that overlap in membership between a focal organization and the organizations in its set will reduce autonomy.

Task environments, as noted by Thompson (1967, pp. 28–30), are multifaceted, pluralistic, and composed of other distinguishable organizations that are relevant in establishing domain consensus and exchanges. This pluralism of task environments means that each focal organization may have to exchange resources with not one but several other organizations, each of which is itself involved with other organizations in networks of interdependence, with its own domain and task environment. It is readily apparent that issues related to domain consensus and/ or resource dependence can result in contingencies to which organizations must respond. For example, during periods of economic decline, a particular community service organization may find that one or several business organizations that previously made contributions are forced to reduce their aid, or other organizations may compete for the scarce resources. Or a new agency, or an agency with a new program for clients, may find itself perceived as "the new kid on the block" who has to justify its existence or aspects of its domain. Two specific issues, the scarcity of resources in the environment and information about the environment needed for decision making, have dominated the literature. Two major perspectives on organization-environment relations have developed that are concerned with these issues.

PERSPECTIVES ON ORGANIZATION-ENVIRONMENT RELATIONS: ENVIRONMENT AS POOL OF RESOURCES AND AS FLOW OF INFORMATION

Aldrich and Mindlin (1978; Aldrich, 1979) have identified two ways of conceptualizing organizational environments: as a pool of resources and as a flow of information. Organizational specialists have tended to adopt one or the other of the two perspectives and have failed to see that they are complementary.

According to the resources conception, the environment is a pool of resources sought by a population of organizations that competes for and shares the resources (Aldrich 1979, pp. 111–122). A particular focal organization's concern may be with organizations that provide resources or with organizations that evaluate or become recipients of the focal organization's outputs (Pennings and Goodman, 1977). Since the resources conception is thought to refer to the objective or "real" environment that exists external to the organization's boundaries, this conception can also take into consideration states of change, complexity, and competition in general environmental conditions. Two theoretical models have developed to explain the resource exchanges that occur between organizations: voluntary resource exchange and resource dependency (Emerson, 1962; Levine and White, 1961, pp. 583, 589–597).

In their study of health and welfare agencies, Levine and White placed great emphasis on voluntary exchanges and defined an exchange as any voluntary activity between two organizatons that has consequences, actual or anticipated, for the realizaton of their respective goals. The main thrust of the Levine and White model is that particular organizations are driven by resource scarcity to enter into exchanges with other organizations.

We will see in the chapter on dyadic interaction that exchanges between organizations are thought to be determined by three related factors: 1. domain consensus, 2. objectives and functions of the organizations, and 3. lack of accessibility to resources from outside the health system. Levine and White's definition of exchange has been criticized by Cook (1977, p. 64), who points out that it is tautological because it includes any form of voluntary activity, rendering the term synonymous with interaction. Cook suggests that the concept exchange should be limited to voluntary transactions involving the transfer of resources between two or more organizations.

A purely environmental perspective is apolitical in the sense that it assumes that resources and information are dispersed in the environment, not concentrated and under the control of some organizations. In contrast, the resource dependence model emphasizes that resources and information may be concentrated. A major consequence of competition for scarce resources is the development of dependencies of some organizations on others. Building upon Emerson's (1962) conception of dependence, one can say that a focal organization is dependent upon a particular organization in its set (1) to the degree that the focal organization's need for resources can be met and (2) in inverse degree to the ability of other organizations to provide the same resources. A major resource dependence hypothesis is that organizations seek to avoid becoming dependent on others and seek to make others dependent on them (Aldrich, 1979, pp. 118–119).

Power is intimately related to dependence. From the resource dependence perspective, potential power is equivalent to the possession of scarce resources. Power in action can be seen as the use of resources to gain the compliance of others (Burt, 1977). In terms of dependence, it should be emphasized (Pfeffer and Salancik, 1978, pp. 50–51) that the critical variable is not the mere concentration of resources or the sheer number of suppliers or purchasers. It is whether or not the focal organization has access to the resources from additional sources that determines dependence. Two major differences between the Levine and White model of exchange and resource dependence can be readily seen: (1) domain consensus is thought to be of minor importance or exist only as a product of exchanges in the resource dependence model and (2) resource exchanges that may not be voluntary are stressed by the resource dependence model.

In contrast to the environment as a pool of available resources, the information conception of environment depicts it as a source of information used by decision makers. This perspective can be seen as supplementing the resource dependence perspective because it focuses upon the processes through which organizational decision makers evaluate the environment, obtain and use feedback about their organization's effectiveness, and take appropriate action. When the environment is seen as a source of information, the most basic concept used has been uncertainty.

While Dill (1958) placed great emphasis on organizations as information-processing systems and on the ways which organizations learn about their environments, Weick (1969) took a quite different view and argued that organizations "create" their environments. From Weick's point of view, it would be said that decision makers in organizations create their environments, develop mental abstractions of them, and then try to adapt to them. Consistent with Weick, Starbuck (1976, pp. 1070–1080) states that an organization first selects those aspects of the environment to which it will relate and then takes appropriate action.

Because of these two different perspectives on the environment as information, we find that some investigators have been most interested in the impact of "objective" environmental characteristics, while others have emphasized "subjective" characteristics or perceived environmental characteristics. What relationships should we expect to find between objective and subjective dimensions of environment? At first glance, logic suggests that in most cases we should expect to find a close correspondence between the two sets of dimensions. But if it is true that members of the organization's dominant coalition selectively, and sometimes poorly, perceive or misread their environment, the relationship between subjective and objective environmental dimensions might be weak and inconsistent.

In the section that follows, we will discuss a typology of potential strategies for managing the environment. By "manage" we mean actions taken to obtain resources and to acquire necessary information. Then, we will discuss and evaluate the weight of the empirical evidence that researchers have assembled to help us understand the interaction between real organizations and their environments—that is, the real strategies used and their impact.

STRATEGIES FOR MANAGING THE ENVIRONMENT

Increasingly, a variety of strategies can be seen at work as focal organizations attempt to relate to their environments. Thompson (1967, pp. 29–36) was among the earliest to point out that organizations may use competitive or cooperative strategies in order to avoid becoming subservient to other organizations. A focal organization may seek alternative sources of resources in order to scatter its dependence. Sometimes, it is possible for a focal organization to acquire prestige, the "cheapest" way to acquire power. For example, an organization may be able to improve its reputation in the community. To the degree that an organization finds it prestigious to relate to a focal organization, the focal organization has acquired a measure of power without making any commitments.

Thompson indicates that cooperative strategies include contracting, coopting, and coalescing, for example, joint ventures or coalitions. Because decision makers value autonomy they will first attempt to use strategies in which the focal organization maintains possession and control over its resources and keeps its boundaries as closed to the influenece of other organizations as possible. Next preferred are strategies requiring cooperation or negotiation with another organization on a dyadic basis. Finally, some sources of interdependence and uncertainty can only be coped with through the joint action of many organizations in action sets. Action sets are thought to develop only when extremely attractive incentives are offered, or when organizations are coerced into participation, or when authorities subscribe to an overarching set of values that emphasize collective action (Aldrich, 1979, pp. 293–317).

It is helpful to categorize alternative strategies in terms of

Figure 3-1. Strategies for Managing Environments

Orientation	Resources	Emphasis	Information
Proactive	1		2
Reactive	3		4

whether they are oriented toward the acquisition of resources in order to reduce the focal organization's dependence, or information in order to reduce its uncertainty. In addition to specifying whether the strategies focus upon resources (dependence) or upon information (uncertainty), it is helpful to categorize them in terms of whether they are proactive or reactive. Four categories of strategies exist (see Figure 3-1).

"Environmental effectiveness" (Metcalf, 1976) is gained through proactive strategies in which the focal organization modifies the environment while "environmental responsiveness" is gained through reactive behavior on the part of the organization as it adjusts itself to given external conditions. A variety of proactive and reactive strategies are discussed by Metcalf. For example, proactive strategies include the formation of developmental coalitions when power is too widely dispersed, and reactive or defensive coalitions to combat the power of a particular organization or existing powerful coalition. Other proactive strategies discussed by Metcalf include seeking alternative resources and abridging exchange relationships. Proactive strategies to reduce uncertainty include making conflicting demands of organization-set members observable to all, promulgating an ideology that is favorable to the focal organization, and creating awareness of convergent interests (conciliatory role) or of conflicting interests (arbitrational role).

Dowling and Pfeffer (1975), in their discussion of organizational legitimacy, point out that an organization might, through proactive communication, try to become identified with symbols, values, or institutions that have a strong base of social legitimacy. Contributing to charity is a legitimizing behavior. Making one's employees or members available to help with community projects also adds to legitimacy. Coopting of various political leaders or of other persons of legitimate status in order to add to the focal organization's status is a proactive strategy. They also indicate that organizations can choose reactive strategies such as adapting their goals, output, or methods of operation to conform to prevailing definitions of legitimacy.

Keep in mind that it is the interest or motivation behind reactive strategies that marks their distinction from proactive ones. Proactive strategies are intended to affect resource exchanges in order to gain relative advantage or to influence the perceived legitimacy of the focal organization. Reactive strategies, on the other hand, may call for modifications in organizational goals, output, or methods in order to guarantee a supply of resources or obtain additional needed information for decisions.

In their analysis Pfeffer and Salancik (1978, pp. 92–110) have also identified strategies that the focal organization can take to reduce the probability of being subject to successful external control. They discuss how dependencies can be avoided or how the conditions of external social control can be managed. For example, a common solution to the potential problem of over-reliance on single sources of resources or markets is to "buffer" the focal organization. Inputs can be developed of sufficient size to reduce the impact of interruptions in resources obtained from a single, or few, sources. To buffer with regard to output, the focal organization can diversify, attempt to gain control over the organizations that provide the needed input, or absorb the focal organization's output. Other proactive strategies (Pfeffer and Salancik, 1978, pp. 188–190, 213) include deliberate efforts by organizatons to use political mechanisms in order to try to create a more favorable environment. Pfeffer and Salancik suggest that organizational attempts to affect the decisions made by government bureaucracies are equally important, if not more so, than their attempts to directly intervene in political elections.

When legitimate strategies are not available, organizations sometimes resort to illegal strategies. Staw and Szwajkowski (1975), in their study of 105 large companies involved in trade litigation from 1968 to 1972, found that the financial performance of cited firms was significantly lower than for other large firms. They concluded that the more scarce the environment, the more likely a firm will engage in illegal acts.

The political influence attempts of interest groups, nonlegislative government bodies, and business and industry on legislation and key legislative policymakers in business and economic matters have been studied and their relative effectiveness determined. Industry and business groups were especially inclined to use an information-based strategy. Nonlegislative government bodies also used an information-based strategy on a frequent basis and seldom used public appeals or public exposure to influence legislative action. Societal interest groups extensively used public exposure and appeals and made greater use of direct contacts with constituents or colleagues of legislators. Which strategies do you think are most effective? A survey of 435 chief legislative assistants in the U.S. House of Representatives during the 95th Congress was conducted to answer this question. It has been concluded that strategies based upon threats of public exposure or direct pressure have relatively less impact than the use of information or the appeal to colleagues or constituents of legislators (Alpin and Hegarty, 1980).

Think for a minute about some particular organization that concerns you. It might be a business, union, school, social service organization, or some other organization. Can you recognize proactive and reactive strategies it has used recently? What were they? What kinds of organizations in your community rely primarily on reactive strategies? Which primarily use proactive ones? You ought to be able to see many examples of strategies at work when you observe television programs, read newspapers, or participate in organizations. Most organizations probably use a combination of proactive and reactive strategies, but some organizations probably have a greater variety of strategies from which to choose.

EMPIRICAL SUPPORT FOR THEORETICAL MODELS

In this section we will analyze some of the empirical research that has been completed. These results will provide us with some basis for evaluating the perspectives and specific propositions we have discussed. The results may also provide some clues as to priority research issues and questions for the 1980s.

The Environment as Information

Let's begin by first examining some of the key propositions suggested by the general model that views environments as a source of information for decision makers. Boundary spanning involves interactions between persons from organizations who interact with persons from other organizations in situations involving both conflict and cooperation. Boundary spanning is thought (Aldrich, 1979, pp. 249–263) to satisfy two functions for the focal organization: information processing and external representation. Information-processing functions include scanning the environment, intelligence gathering, and protecting the organization against information overload. External representation functions include resource acquisition and disposal and maintaining or improving the organization's political legitimacy and image.

Efforts have been made to integrate the literature and to identify variables that are thought to be associated with boundary spanning (Aldrich and Herker, 1977; Leifer and Delbecq, 1978). It is thought that organizations that utilize a technology involving uncertainty will emphasize relatively more boundary spanning. Organizations in environments where important elements are concentrated—in heterogeneous environments, in rapidly changing environments, and in lean environments—will emphasize boundary spanning in order to reduce uncertainty. In addition, it is thought that boundary spanning will be emphasized most by organizations with inadequate internal memory and by organizations with diverse or unclear goals than by organizations with singular or unambiguous goals.

Lawrence and Lorsch's (1967a) and Duncan's (1972) famous studies in which they developed scales to measure perceived environmental uncertainty (PEU) are frequently cited. They concluded after their research that environmental change and complexity causes uncertainty.

These early PEU studies were criticized immediately. Hall (1968) pointed out that Lawrence and Lorsch had provided no information on the causal mechanisms by which environmental influences enter the organization. Two recent studies (Downey, Hellriegel, and Slocum, 1975; Tosi, Aldag, and Storey, 1973) of managers in business have been particularly critical of scales developed by Lawrence and Lorsch and Duncan. The two studies found that PEU subscale scores were not significantly correlated with each other, which means that the subscale scores were not reliable instruments. In addition, and quite distressing from a contingency point of view, most of the subscale PEU scores were not significantly correlated with objective measures of the environment.

Leifer and Huber (1977) indicate that boundary-spanning activities can be seen as an intervening variable standing between organizational structure and PEU. Boundary spanners operate at the "skin of the organization," with their function being to interpret environmental conditions and relay that information to decision makers. This particular study by Leifer and Huber is important because it is one of the few studies in which propositions linking PEU, boundary spanning, and organizational structure were developed and evaluated with empirical data.

Perceptions of organicism (flexibility of structure), uncertainty (PEU), and extent of boundary spanning for subjects were analyzed. Positive relationships were found between the three variables that measured PEU, organicism, and boundary-spanning activity. However, the relationship between organicism and PEU disappeared when boundary spanning was controlled, and the relationship between PEU and boundary spanning disappeared when organicism was controlled. It was concluded that organicism influenced boundary-spanning activity to a greater extent than did PEU. This implies that inasmuch as structure is an administratively controlled variable, the amount of PEU admitted at the boundary of the organization may be administratively controlled. The data could also be used to support the argument that organicism (flexibility of structure) influences boundary spanning, which influences PEU. The researchers conclude that the role of the boundary spanner as a mediator between environmental influences and organization structure may still be supported, and the importance of the boundary-spanning function to organization theory is underscored.

Studies by Pennings (1975) and Schmidt and Cummings (1976) have examined the relationship between objective and subjective environmental dimensions, and these studies did not support the prediction that objective and subjective variables are related. Betty Wells (1980), in a study of managers of farmer cooperatives, reported positive but very low correlations between measures of PEU and boundary spanning. Mulford, Tillotson, Klonglan, and Warren (1980) have completed a study of county units of university extension in which a variety of measures of boundary-spanning activities were analyzed in relation to perceived environmental change, competition, and uncertainty. Most of the correlations reported were low and insignificant.

Aldrich (1979, p. 157) has suggested that researchers should not be overly surprised or concerned if the correlations between objective and subjective variables are only moderately strong. Resource constraints and negative feedback from misperceptions may eventually direct perceptions toward congruence with reality. In addition, relative, not absolute, accuracy is all that may be needed to guide organizational adaptation. Pfeffer and Salancik (1978, pp. 78–82) suggest that the organization is in a sense always lagging: its attentional processes are inevitably focused upon what has been important in the past, and the objective environment is changing. Perhaps we should not expect to find significant correlations between perceived and objective dimensions.

Although organizational decisions and actions may be determined by the "enacted environment," through the strategic choices available to the dominant coalition, problems can arise if mechanisms operate that screen out information and protect the organization from external influences. For example, Pfeffer and Salancik point out that the Nixon White House had an elaborate filtering system protecting its occupant from external information. Problems can also arise if the dominant coalition misreads its situation of interdependence, or the demands made on it, or of resolving conflicting demands.

The Environment as a Pool of Available Resources

The environment as resources model has motivated a great deal of empirical research. Some of the earliest research in this

tradition was conducted in order to evaluate the relative importance of voluntary resource exchange theory as developed by
Levine and White (1961) compared to the resource dependence
theory discussed earlier in this chapter.

Adamek and Lavin (1969) used data from a study with 321
health and welfare agencies located in 60 Ohio counties to test
Levine and White's proposition that resource scarcity drives particular organizations to develop exchange relations. The researchers found just the opposite. Those organizations with the
most resources were most likely to refer clients to other organizations and participate in case conferences. Litwak and Rothman (1970) report similar findings in a study of Detroit schools,
and so do Klonglan, Dillman, Wright, and Beal (1969) in a study
of alcoholism service agencies.

Adamek and Lavin conclude that their study results do not
completely deny the importance of the scarcity hypothesis, but
it may apply best at the community subsystem level. In other
words, widespread resource scarcity within a subsystem may lead
to more frequent exchanges within the subsystem. But, for particular organizations, resource scarcity is negatively associated
with frequency of exchanges. In related research, Mulford and
Mulford (1977) report that voluntary organizations that are
larger and have greater output (sponsor more activities for the
community) are more likely to engage in cooperation with other
voluntary organizations.

Aiken and Hage's (1968) study with 16 social welfare and
health organizations is frequently referenced in the literature
because of its contributions to the resource dependence model.
In this study Aiken and Hage posited that with an increase in
division of labor, organizations become more complex and more
innovative. The need for resources to support such innovations
leads to joint programs with other organizations and contributes
to greater community integration. It was found that organizations
with more joint programs tend to be more complex and innovative and have more internal communication and somewhat
more decentralized decision-making structures.

Because the sample of organizations was so small in the Aik-
en and Hage study, replication of this study was important.

Paulson (1974) extended the theory proposed by Aiken and Hage by developing a causal model of organizational determinants of joint programs in his study of 138 health and welfare organizations. Paulson's results largely supported Aiken and Hage's model. In particular, Paulson found a significant correlation between innovations and joint programs.

The study by Mulford and Mulford (1981) is important in that Aiken and Hage's model was evaluated with data from a study of voluntary organizations in three different communities. Through the use of available survey and census data, the Mulfords suggested that it was possible to at least nominally categorize the three communities on a scale of environmental turbulence from low to medium to high. All of the voluntary organizations in the three communities were included in the study. The results shown in Table 3-1 are abstracted from the Mulfords' study.

Note that the number of program innovations were significantly and positively associated with the number of joint programs for Urban A, the county seat community; but the number of previous joint programs was a much better correlate of current joint programs for *each* of the communities. Innovations were not significantly correlated with joint programs in Rural B, which was described as intermediate to the other two communities with regard to turbulence. Innovations are significantly and positively correlated with conflict in Rural C, and there is a trend for innovative organizations to have fewer joint programs. These results can be interpreted to mean that the Aiken and Hage model works best in a stable and nonturbulent environment. Voluntary organizations that are innovative in a turbulent environment appear to threaten other organizations, and joint programs are not as likely.

Mileti and Gillespie (1976) have integrated considerable literature and developed a general model of organizational changes induced by environmental forces. Gillespie and Mileti (1979) have observed that two alternative models exist for explaining organization-environment relations, namely one in which organizations are viewed as adapting to environmental changes, and a second model in which organizations are viewed as actively manipulating environments. Gillespie and Mileti state that empirical

Table 3-1. Zero-Order Coefficients of Correlation Between Organizational Variables and Joint Programs, and Conflict for Three Communities

Organizational Variables:	Urban A The County Seat Low Turbulence		Rural B A Small Community Medium Turbulence		Rural C A Small Community High Turbulence	
	Joint Programs	Conflict	Joint Programs	Conflict	Joint Programs	Conflict
1. No. of Program Innovations	.331*	−.001	.172	−.112	−.219	.444*
2. No. of Previous Joint Programs	.669*	.207*	.719*	−.080	.316*	−.108

*Significant at the .05 level

appraisals are needed to evaluate these alternative compatible models.

In their research with 27 heterogeneous business corporations, Gillespie and Mileti sought to determine if it made more sense to conceptualize corporate organizational structure as dependent upon environments or to see the structure as determining relations with the environment. Their overall results led them to conclude that environmental processes may have as strong an effect on determining corporate structure as structure has on determining environmental processes. They suggest that future research models should construct and test nonrecursive models in order to gauge the simultaneous effects upon one another.

Some of the specific results from the study by Gillespie and Mileti (1979, pp. 268–269) are quite interesting in terms of our discussions here. They found that organizations with the most assets and the most routine technology exert the least effort in attempting to manipulate their environments. They conclude that success in a competitive corporate world requires some expenditures of organizational effort to direct environments in favor of the organization, but relative success decreases the need to divert environments in favor of the organization. Relative success also decreases the need to divert environments in order to maintain that position of success.

Aveni (1978) has proposed that both the strength and breadth of linkages with other organizations may be important for an overall framework of resource mobilization. Aveni suggested that the concepts of "linkage strength" and "linkage breadth" provided one possible explanation for the strong influence of the NAACP. Whetten and Aldrich (1979) have indicated that the size and diversity of organization sets for people-processing organizations, such as manpower organizations, are critical for effectiveness because the linkages between organizations serve as lifelines through which the resources necessary to implement an organization's core technology are received. Incidentally, Whetten and Aldrich found in their study of 64 manpower organizations that some of the best predictors of set size and diversity are variables over which local administrators have little control, such as the number of organizations in their community, the local budget, number of staff and number of services offered to clients. In a similar argument, Warren (1974) has proposed that the effectiveness of new local health delivery systems is directly affected by interorganizational linkages.

What does the limited available research indicate with regard to these propositions about effectiveness? Paulson (1974) reported small and nonsignificant correlations between goal accomplishments and the number of joint programs in his study with 138 health and welfare organizations. Osborn and Hunt (1974), who completed an analysis of the reported goal achievement of 26 small, rigidly structured social service organizations, found that an indirect measure of interaction with other organizations was associated with effectiveness. Mulford, Warren, Klonglan, Tillotson, Ganey, and Kopachevsky (1979), in their analysis of the goal attainment of 461 local disaster planning organizations, found that the number of linkages with private sector organizations was positively and significantly correlated with effectiveness. Among the findings reported by Mulford et al. goal achievement was positively and significantly correlated with linkages used to secure audiences to hear about the need for disaster planning, linkages that resulted in resource exchanges and exchanges of members for advisory boards of committees. In summary, these available studies do indicate some support for the notion that linkages with other organizations in an organization's immediate environment may impact an organization's effectiveness.

Boards of directors are thought to be important because the members may provide linkages to other organizations and access to resources and legitimacy. Zald (1967) has reported from his study of 34 branches of the YMCA that high-status boards contribute greater financial aid and are associated with departments rated as more effective in program quality, level of efficiency, and board strength. On the other hand, higher-status boards show lower meeting attendance rates and less participation in programs.

Pfeffer (1972) has found that the size and composition of boards of directors of 80 corporations was related to economic performance. Pfeffer reported that deviations from optimal board composition, based on the average for the 80 corporations, were negatively related to the ratio of net income to jobs and the ratio of net income to stockholders equity. Pfeffer (1973, pp. 361–362) has found in his study of 57 hospitals that the size of hospital boards, as predicted, tended to be larger the larger the hospital budget, the larger the proportion of funds obtained from private donations, and the more important "influence in the community" and "fund raising" were as criteria for selecting board members. Boards of directors selected for fund raising rather than for administration, and boards that more closely fit their environment, tended to be associated with effectiveness, measured by additions in programs and services, percentage increase in number of beds, and percentage increase in the budget. These studies confirm the important role of boards of directors for effectiveness.

The Contingency Model of Effectiveness

Contingency theory is the dominant model of organizational effectiveness today. Going beyond a discussion of strategies for managing the environment, contingency theory asks us to think about the kind of organizatonal structure required for effectiveness. For this model's perspective, there is no best way for structuring an organization. Instead, it is thought that the internal structure required for effectiveness depends upon the nature of the organization's environment.

Burns and Stalker (1961) were among the very first to analyze relationships between organizations and their environment from a contingency perspective. They observed that 20 British industrial firms could be distinguished from one another on the basis of their organizational structure. "Mechanistic" organizations were characterized by high degrees of task differentiation, formalization, centralization of decision making, vertical communication and low professionalization. These organizations had relatively closed and inflexible structures. "Organic" organizations, on the other hand, had flexible and open structures.

Burns and Stalker reasoned that mechanistic structures

seemed to be most appropriate for firms operating in relatively stable and predictable environments. Mechanistic structures were thought to be less effective if firms operated in environments characterized by change and flux because mechanistic structures impede the free flow of communication and decision making. Organic systems appeared to be more appropriate under the latter environmental conditions.

In summary, they proposed that an organic organizational structure will be associated with organizational effectiveness under conditions of environmental change and a mechanistic structure will be associated with organizational effectiveness under conditions of environmental stability. The contingency perspective stands in strong contrast with Max Weber's classical organizational theory (Weber, 1947) that sought the best structural arrangements for effectiveness.

Influenced by Burns and Stalker, Lawrence and Lorsch (1967a, 1967b) sought to more vigorously test some of the contingency hypotheses. Six organizations in a plastics industry and four in the container industry were selected for study. The environment of the plastics industry was characterized by rapid technological and market change, high complexity, and high uncertainty, while the container industry was selected because its environment was the polar opposite. Lawrence and Lorsch reported that the more highly effective organizations operating in the unstable, complex, and uncertain environments were highly differentiated, with each unit dealing with only a portion of the total environment. They used special integrative devices, including integrating teams, and an emphasis on direct contact among managers at all levels, instead of relying on integration through rules and the hierarchy. Effective organizations operating in less turbulent environments had less differentiation and relied upon rules and the hierarchy for intergration.

Two approaches for evaluating contingency theory can be identified in recent literature. Some persons have sought to determine what, if any, direct effects environments have on organizational structure. We have already referred to the study by Leifer and Huber (1977) in which they investigated relationships between organic structure, perceived environmental uncertainty, and extent of boundary-spanning activity. Remember they concluded that organicism (structure) had a greater effect on boundary-spanning activity than environmental uncertainty.

What kinds of environments are thought to have greater effects on organizational structure? In his study of 72 morning newspapers published in 67 metropolitan centers, DuBick (1978) asserts that newspapers become differentiated and specialized when they are located in nationally dominant cities, metropolitan leisure services are more abundant, the population is largely middle and upper middle class, the population is more racially and occupationally heterogeneous, and competition between newspapers is higher. The most important finding, however, from DuBick's work is that the relationship (the "fit") between environmental variables and organizational structure was stronger for those newspapers operating in a competitive environment. Newspapers appear to have considerable operating discretion when competition is absent, and noncompetitive newspapers appear not to be structurally responsive to a wide range of public interests. Indeed, noncompetitive newspapers may well be acting as information filters rather than as information disseminators.

DuBick's decision to analyze the relationships between environmental variables separately for newspapers that operated in a competitive environment and for newspapers that did not was crucial for his analysis. Had DuBick not done this, he would not have found any significant relationships between environmental and structural variables. Pennings and Tripathi (1978) also sought to determine if relationships existed between certainty-uncertainty environmental dimensions and bureaucratic-nonbureaucratic dimensions in their analysis of 40 widely dispersed offices of a U.S. brokerage firm. They wished to test the proposition that organizations will be participative, power equalized, and informationally intergrated if their domain is disputed, uncertain, and ill-understood. Most of the relationships reported by Pennings and Tripathi are low and not significant. It is interesting to wonder if controlling on a significant dimension of environment would have aided in their analysis as it did for DuBick.

One frequently finds implications in the literature that organizational effectiveness is at least partly determined by the environment. Nevertheless, relatively few studies have been completed that focus specifically upon the part that the environment plays in the effectiveness of organizations. Hirsch (1975) has found that the typical pharmaceutical manufacturing firm is more profitable than the typical phonograph record company because of greater control over its environment. The typical pharmaceutical firm has greater control over pricing and distribution, greater access to patents and more favorable copyright laws, and has been more successful in coopting external opinion leaders than has the typical phonograph record company. While Hirsch's study is helpful, it tells us little about particular organizations and their effectiveness. Let's turn at this point to an analysis of one of the few empirical studies that have looked at characteristics of environments and the effectiveness of specific organizations.

Empirical studies of the impact of environmental dimensions on effectiveness are rare indeed. Although Tillotson's (1980, pp. 123–124, 197) major goal in her research was to integrate the literature on contingency models of effectiveness and to evaluate the integrated model, she does report correlations between general environmental variables and organizational effectiveness. Tillotson used the evaluation of higher level administrators, elected officials, and clients of 99 county units of university extension for measures of goal achievement. She used objective environmental variables (environmental change, complexity, and competition), and subjective environmental variables in her analysis. Tillotson reports that objective environmental competition for clients, perceived competition, and perceived environmental uncertainty were significantly and negatively related to two or more of the three measures of organizational effectiveness.

The second perspective on contingency theory fits the original conceptions of Burns and Stalker (1961), namely, that the appropriate structure for effectiveness depends upon the organization's environment.

Surprisingly, given its importance in the literature, very few empirical studies have been designed to specifically test contingency theory as formulated by Burns and Stalker. Let's analyze three recent studies designed for this purpose. Neghandi and Reimann (1972) have analyzed 30 manufacturing firms in India; Pennings (1975) used data from 40 branch offices of a U.S. brokerage firm; and Child (1975) used data from a sample of 81 British business firms. To what extent do these studies support contingency theory? Neghandi and Reimann (1972) found a positive and significant correlation between decentralized decision making and organizational effectiveness despite the relatively stable task environment in India. Pennings found that consistency between environmental and structural variables had little bearing on organizational effectiveness. Child tested the contingency hypothesis that stated that the most successful companies in unstable environments have more specialization and less formalization. Child's findings supported the hypothesis for formalization and one measure of effectiveness but did not support the hypothesis for specialization.

Tillotson's (1980) efforts are among the latest conducted to evaluate the contingency model. Tillotson completed an intensive analysis using both objective and subjective environmental variables. Tillotson sought to determine if organizations with an organic structure are more effective in turbulent environments and if organizations with a mechanistic structure are more effective in less turbulent environments. The fate of Tillotson's study was comparable to that of other contingency studies. Almost no aspect of contingency theory was supported. Despite these results, contingency theory remains a very important influence in the literature.

SUMMARY

The environments of organizations, especially their task environments, can be seen as sources of constraints and contingencies for decision makers. Two general and complementary perspectives have been developed to conceptualize organization-environment relations, namely, the environment conceived of as information or as a pool of available resources. Relations between organizations and their environments do not occur on a one-way street. That is, to at least some extent, an organization's dominant coalition enacts its environment. Both proactive and reactive strategies exist for managing environments, and most organizations probably use a combination of strategies to obtain resources and information for decision making.

An assessment of the limited available empirical research indicates that larger organizations, with more resources and more activities, are more likely than others to establish joint programs. Organizations that are more innovative are more likely to establish joint programs, perhaps to help pay for the costs of innovations. Innovations may lead to conflict with other organizations in turbulent environments if they are seen as threats. Environments can also function in ways that make innovations in organizations more likely.

Boundary-spanning activities are thought to satisfy two functions for organizations: information-processing and external representation. Empirical research indicates that boundary-spanning functions are not well understood in terms of their relationships with structural variables and perceived environmental uncertainty. Perceptions of the environment are very poorly correlated with objective environmental dimensions.

To at least a modest degree, the literature suggests that effective use of strategies to manage environments is associated with organizational effectiveness. The strength and breadth of linkages with other organizations are frequently discussed in terms of their impact on effectiveness, and the size and composition of boards have received considerable attention.

In defense of contingency theory, it is true that only a few empirical studies have been conducted, and these are all cross-sectional with small samples of organizations. More research is clearly needed. Models of organizations will not be complete until they include a comprehensive understanding of strategies for managing environments and contingent considerations with regard to structure.

Bourgeois, McAllister, and Mitchell (1978) pose an especially knotty issue for contingency theory advocates. Many of today's managers have not been exposed to contingency theory ideas. If turbulent environments cause uncertainty, might managers actually attempt to "pull in the reins" and reduce the uncertainty by resorting to a mechanistic structure instead of an organic structure? In a contrived laboratory study, it was found that individuals actually responded more organically to stable environments and more mechanistically to turbulent environments. These subjects shifted to a more mechanistic mode when turbulence followed stability, but they did not shift to a more organic mode when the environment became more stable.

What can be done if these results are typical? Bourgeois, et al. indicate that one option calls for additional training and development for managers to increase their abilities to enact organic states at appropriate times. The other possibility is for contingency theorists to recognize and fully appreciate the role of managerial choice in not seeking a goodness of fit between organizations and their environments. Once a certain minimum level of effectiveness is reached, managerial inclinations and values may take precedence over either technological or environmental contingencies. To the degree that these "irrational" motives and strategies exist, they must be incorporated into our explanation of organizations and their environments.

Many interesting questions about organizations and their environments have been at least partly answered, but many remain. In particular, longitudinal research with organizations in a variety of community settings is needed. Even after this research has been done, we will still have an incomplete view. Studies with particular organizations will be able to tell us which organizations are most likely to interact with others, but this research will not tell us "with whom" they will interact. The "with whom" questions can only be answered by taking a dyadic perspective. Models developed to understand dyadic relations and the empirical research that has been conducted to evaluate these models are presented in the next chapter.

Discussion Questions

1. What roles do dominant coalitions play in organizations?

2. How does Thompson's concept "organizational rationality" differ from technical rationality?

3. How do the characteristics of an organization's set affect the organization's autonomy? Give examples from your community.

4. Compare and contrast conceptions of the environment as resources and as information.

5. How do proactive strategies differ from reactive ones? Give examples from your community.

6. What role is boundary-spanning activity thought to play in reducing PEU?

7. How can the lack of correlation between objective and subjective environment variables be explained?

8. Why are organizations that are more innovative more likely to establish joint programs?

9. Evaluate the research results completed to determine if proactive strategies add to an organization's effectiveness.

10. How does the contingency model of effectiveness differ from Max Weber's model? What work is needed in order to more fully evaluate contingency theory?

A FICTITIOUS CASE STUDY: THE NEW DIRECTOR

The past week, his first week on the job, has certainly been less than spectacular for Will Jones, the newly appointed Director of County Social Services for Brown County. The main problem seems to be that everything is happening at once in the agency, and Will Jones is unfamiliar with the county, having just moved there from another state. The Assistant Director (Sue Wood) is also new to the agency and Will can't rely upon Sue for the immediate help that he needs.

Brown County is growing rapidly, partly because it is adjacent to the county containing the state capitol, and the number of staff in the agency has been increased to handle the increased workload. Both county and state officials who were involved in hiring Jones made it perfectly clear that they expected positive results now that the number of agency staff had been increased and an Assistant Director hired too.

Unfortunately, the agency's budget is still too small, and it is already obvious to Jones that, even with the increased staff, it will be difficult for the agency to meet all of its goals. A large number of aged persons reside in the county, and they are especially hard to reach in rural areas and in the smaller towns. Despite its rich agricultural base and the relatively high earnings of employed workers, many poor families do exist. In addition to the existence of many clients and potential clients, other problems exist too. The state has mandated that County Social Services, Area Agencies on Aging, and Local Mental Health Centers will coordinate their planning for the delivery of services. Unfortunately, no guidelines have been provided for implementing this mandate. Will Jones hasn't even met the administrators of these agencies yet, and he isn't anxious to do so. Jones is afraid that his agency's work and responsibilities will suffer if he and his staff have to take on other less essential work. Jones knows that his budget is probably larger than the budget of the Area Agency on Aging or the budget of the Local Mental Health Center, which means that they need him, he reasons, more than he needs them. Jones knows, too, that the federal funds his agency receives are clearly earmarked for specific services for clients and agency activities and he must check to be certain that federal rules are not violated when, and if, relationships are established with the aging and the mental health agencies.

Jones and Wood decide upon a two-pronged strategy for becoming familiar with their agency and for program planning. Wood will review current case loads with agency staff and be briefed by program leaders. She will, in turn, brief Jones on a weekly basis. Jones will review all existing contractual and informal arrangements that exist with other agencies in the county and he will become more familiar with the recent state mandate. After Jones' preliminary analysis is complete, the two administrators will be able to determine which linkages with other agencies are most helpful and if any should be terminated. Some action with regard to the new state mandate can also be considered at that time.

QUESTIONS FOR CASE ANALYSIS

1. What advice would you give to Jones and Wood about the situation? What criteria are most relevant for evaluating the success of linkages with other agencies?
2. What would you suggest if, indeed, the new mandate is somewhat vague and unclear with regard to its implementation?
3. What impact, if any, will adherence to the mandate have upon the operation of their agency?

REFERENCES

Adamek, R. J., & Lavin, B. F. Interorganizational exchange: A note on the scarcity hypothesis. In A. R. Neghandi (Ed.), *Interorganizational theory*. Kent, OH: Kent State University Press, 1969, pp. 196–210.

Aiken, M., & Hage, J. Organizational interdependence and intraorganizational structure. *American Sociological Review*, 1968, *33*, 912–930.

Aldrich, H. E. *Organizations and environments*. Englewood Cliffs, NJ: Prentice-Hall, 1979.

Aldrich, H. E., & Herker, D. Boundary spanning roles and organizational structure. *The Academy of Management Review*, 1977, *2*, 217–230.

Aldrich, H. E., & Mindlin, S. Uncertainty and dependence: Two perspectives on environments. In L. Karpik (Ed.), *Organization and environment*. Beverly Hills, CA: Sage Publications, Inc., 1978.

Alpin, J. C., & Hegarty, W. H. Political influence: Strategies employed by organizations to impact legislation in business and economic matters. *Academy of Management Journal*, 1980, *23*, 438–450.

Aveni, A. F. Organizational linkages and resource mobilization: The significance of linkage strength and breadth. *Sociological Quarterly*, 1978, *19*, 185–202.

Bourgeois, L. J., III, McAllister, D., & Mitchell, T. R. The effects of different organizational environments upon decisions about organizational structure. *Academy of Management Journal*, 1978, *21*, 508–514.

Burns, T., & Stalker, G. M. *The management of innovation*. London: Tavistock Publications, 1961.

Burt, R. S. Power in a social typology. *Social Science Research*, 1977, *6*, 1–83.

Child, J. Organizational structure, environment and performance: The role of strategic choice. *Sociology*, 1972, *6*, 1–22.

————Managerial and organizational factors associated with company performance: Part II. A contingency analysis. *Journal of Management Studies*, 1975, *12*, 12–27.

Cook, K. S. Exchange and power in networks of interorganizatonal relations. *Sociological Quarterly*, 1977, *18*, 62–82.

Dill, W. R. Environment as an influence on managerial autonomy. *Administrative Science Quarterly*, 1958, *2*, 409–443.

Dowling, J., & Pfeffer, J. Organizational legitimacy. *Pacific Sociological Review*, 1975, *18*, 122–136.

Downey, H. K., Hellriegel, D., & Slocum, J. M., Jr. Individual characteristics as sources of perceived uncertainty variability. *Human Relations*, 1975, *30*, 161–174.

DuBick, M. A. The organizational structure of newspapers in relation to their metropolitan environments. *Administrative Science Quarterly*, 1978, *23*, 418–433.

Duncan, R. B. Characteristics of organizational, environments and perceived environmental uncertainty. *Administrative Science Quarterly*, 1972, *17*, 313–327.

Emerson, R. M. Power-dependence relations. *American Sociological Review*, 1962, *27*, 31–40.

Evan, W. M. Toward a theory of interorganizational relations. *Management Science*, 1965, *11*, No. 10, 217–231.

Gillespie, D. F., & Mileti, D. S. Action and contingency postulates in organization-environment relations. *Human Relations*, 1979, *32*, 261–271.

Hall, R. H. Professionalism and bureaucratization. *American Sociological Review*, 1968, *33*, 92–104.

————*Organizations: Structure and process*, Englewood Cliffs, NJ: Prentice-Hall, 1977.

Hirsch, P. M. Organizational effectiveness and the institutional environment. *Administrative Science Quarterly*, 1975, *20*, 327–344.

Klonglan, G. E., Dillman, D. A., Wright, J. S., & Beal G. M. *Agency interaction patterns and community alcoholism services.* Ames, IA: Department of Sociology and Anthropology, Iowa State University, 1969.

Lawrence, P. R., & Lorsch, J. W. Differentiation and integration in complex organizations. *Administrative Science Quarterly*, 1967a, *12*, 1–18.

————*Organizational environment: Managing differentiation and integration.* Homewood, IL: Richard D. Irwin, 1967b.

Leifer, R., & Delbecq, A. Organizational environmental interchange: A model of boundary spanning activity. *Academy of Management Review*, 1978, *3*, 40–50.

Leifer, R., & Huber, G. P. Relations among perceived environmental uncertainty, organizational structure, and boundary-spanning activity. *Administrative Science Quarterly*, 1977, *22*, 235–247.

Levine, S. & White, P. E. Exchange as a conceptual framework for the study of interorganizational relationships. *Administrative Science Quarterly*, 1961, *5*, 583–610.

Litwak, E., & Rothman, J. Toward the theory and practice of coordination between formal organizations. In W. R. Rosengren & M. Lefton (Eds.), *Organizations and clients.* Columbus, OH: Charles E. Merrill, 1970, pp. 137–186.

Metcalf, J. L. Organizational strategies and interorganizational networks. *Human Relations*, 1976, *29*, 327–343.

Mileti, D. S., & Gillespie, D. F. An intergrated formalization of organization-environment interdependencies. *Human Relations*, 1976, *29*, No. 1, 85–100.

Mulford, C. L., & Mulford, M. A. Community and interorganizational perspectives on cooperation and conflict. *Rural Sociology*, 1977, *42*, 569–590.

Mulford, C. L., & Mulford, M. A. Interorganizational relationships in three communities: Implications for community development. Unpublished paper, Department of Sociology, Iowa State University, Ames, IA, 1981.

Mulford, C. L., Tillotson, L. M., Klonglan, G. E., & Warren, R. D. Congruent or complementary dimensions: Relationships between subjective and objective environmental variables. Unpublished paper, Department of Sociology, Iowa State University, Ames, IA, 1980.

Mulford, C. L., Warren, R. D., Klonglan, G. E., Tillotson, L. M., Ganey, R. F., & Kopachevsky, J. P. Interorganizational relations and goal achievement. Unpublished paper, Department of Sociology, Iowa State University, Ames, IA: July, 1979.

Neghandi, A. R., & Reimann, B. C. A contingency theory of organization re-examined in the context of a developing country. *Academy of Management Journal*, 1972, *15*, 137–146.

Osborn, R. N., & Hunt, J. A. Environment and organizational effectiveness. *Administrative Science Quarterly*, 1974, *19*, 231–245.

Paulson, S. K. Causal analysis of interorganizational relations: An axiomatic theory. *Administrative Science Quarterly*, 1974, *19*, 319–337.

Pennings, J. M. The relevance of the structural contingency model for organizational effectiveness. *Administrative Science Quarterly*, 1975, *20*, 393–407.

Pennings, J. M., & Goodman, P. S. Toward a framework of organizational effectiveness. In P. S. Goodman, J. M. Pennings, and associates (Eds.), *New perspectives on organizational effectiveness*. San Francisco: Jossey-Bass, 1977.

Pennings, J. M., & Tripathi, R. C. The organization-environment relationship: Dimensional versus typological viewpoints. In L. Karpik (Ed.), *Organizations and Environment*. Beverly Hills, CA: Sage Publications, Inc., 1978, pp. 171–195.

Pfeffer, J. Size and composition of corporate boards of direction: The organization and its environment. *Administrative Science Quarterly*, 1972, *17*, 218–228.

————Size, composition, and function of hospital boards of directors: A study of organization-environment linkage. *Administrative Science Quarterly*, 1973, *18*, 349–363.

Pfeffer, J., & Salancik, G. R. *The external control of organizations*. New York: Harper and Row, 1978.

Schmidt, S. M., & Cummings, L. Organizational environment, differentiation and perceived environmental uncertainty. *Decision Sciences*, 1976, *7*, 447–467.

Starbuck, W. H. Organizations and their environments. In M. D. Dunnett (Ed.), *Handbook of industrial and organizational psychology*. Chicago: Rand McNally, 1976.

Staw, B. M., & Szwajkowski, E. The scarcity—munificence component of organizational environments and the commission of illegal acts. *Administrative Science Quarterly*, 1975, *20*, 345–354.

Thompson, J. D. *Organizations in action*. New York: McGraw-Hill, 1967.

Tillotson, L. M. *Toward a contingency theory of organizational effectiveness*. Unpublished Ph.D. dissertation, Department of Sociology, Iowa State University, Ames, IA, 1980.

Tosi, H., Aldag, R., & Storey, R. On the measurement of environment: An assessment of the Lawrence and Lorsch environment uncertainty subscale. *Administrative Science Quarterly*, 1973, *18*, 27–36.

Warren, J. T. The Effects of Interorganizational Linkages on Organizational Survival: An Ecological Analysis of a New Health Care Delivery System. Paper presented at the Organization and Occupations Section of the American Sociological Society Meetings, Montreal, Canada, 1974.

Weber, M. *The theory of social and economic organization*. Translated and edited by A. M. Henderson and T. Parsons. New York: Oxford University Press, 1947.

Weick, K. E. *The social psychology of organizing.* Reading: Addison-Wesley, 1969.

Wells, B. L. *Directing rural cooperatives in uncertain environments.* Unpublished Ph.D. dissertation, Iowa State University, Ames, IA, 1980.

Whetten, D. A., & Aldrich, H. E. Organization set size and diveristy. *Administration and Society,* 1979, *11,* 251–281.

Zald, M. N. Urban differentiation, characteristics of boards of directors, and organizational effectiveness. *American Journal of Sociology,* 1967, *73,* 261–272.

Chapter 4

INTERACTION BETWEEN ORGANIZATIONS

Factors Affecting Dyadic Relations

Consider activities in one community that relate to the needs of young persons. The high school encourages students who are looking for work after school to contact the local employment agency. The juvenile court decides to refer juveniles in trouble with the law to a local shelter house and instructs the probation staff to jointly plan treatment programs with the shelter house staff. A local mental health center signs a contract with the shelter house to provide psychological testing services for youth. In order to promote greater communication and understanding of each other's programs, several organizations concerned with youth decide to exchange board or committee members.

But conflict exists in the community, too. Some differences in philosophy exist between shelter house staff and local police, and the city council and county board of supervisors disagree over funding responsibilities for youth programs. While we are no less interested in the activities of particular organizations that serve youth, few of us can fail to see that these interorganizational decisions to cooperate and the conflict that exists between organizations will have an impact on programs for youth. For similar reasons, it is very necessary for us to understand dyadic relations between organizations in other subsystems of the community and between organizations located at local, state, and federal levels.

Paulson (1976, pp. 311–313) has pointed out that the forces that bring an organization to interact with other organizations are not the same as those that will determine "with whom" the organization will interact; furthermore, we know much less about the latter than the former. We will see in this chapter that few studies of dyads have been completed as compared to studies of particular organizations.

Studies of interaction in dyads, and the factors that influence the interaction, can be contrasted with the more predominant organizational and full systemic approaches that describe entire networks of interacting organizations. A concern for particular organizations, for dyadic relations, and for network studies may be seen as stages in the development of IOR theory and guidelines for persons with applied interest in community development. A concern for dyads of organizations can be seen as a link between studies of particular organizations and larger systems.

We have seen in the previous chapter that resource scarcity and the need for information for decision making are powerful forces that may induce particular organizations to enter into resource exchanges with other organizations (even if this means that they will suffer some loss in autonomy) and to place greater effort on environmental scanning. Our goal here is to better understand the flow of resources and information between organizations in dyads. We are interested in two specific questions:

1. What kinds of resources and information flow between organizations?
2. What kinds of variables are associated with interaction?

We have observed (Figure 2-3) that our attention is drawn to comparative properties, relational properties, and linkage mechanisms between organizations when we analyze dyadic interaction. The number and kinds of linkage mechanisms and conflict that occur are the dependent variables in our analysis.

The various comparative properties (such as homogeneity of structure and function, awareness of other parties, stability, size, and philosophies) and relational properties (such as intensity, reciprocity, standardization, and formalization) are used as independent variables.

THOERETICAL MODELS OF DYADIC RELATIONS

Two overarching perspectives have been developed to explain aspects of environment-organizational relations: a perspective that views the environment as a pool of available resources, and a second perspective that views the environment as a pool of information. Although we have already discussed these two perspectives and related organizational strategies in some detail (see Chapter 3), let's review for a moment some of the key elements in these two perspectives.

Aldrich and Pfeffer (1976) have indicated that theorists take at least two somewhat distinct approaches to conceptualizing environment-organizational relations. One group of theorists (e.g., Dill, 1958; Duncan, 1972: Weick, 1969) treats an organization's environment as a pool of information perceived by members at the boundaries. A second group of theorists (e.g., Aiken and Hage, 1968; Levine and White, 1961; Pennings, 1975) treats an organization's environment as a pool of available resources. When the environment is treated as a source of information, the basic concept used is uncertainty; decision makers are uncertain because they lack information. In contrast, when the pool of available resources perspective is used, dependence becomes the dominant concept, and other related concepts such as resource exchange, input and output transactions, and control over resources are stressed.

Aldrich (1979, pp. 106–135) points out that the two perspectives are complementary and that questions about resource dependence and uncertainty are equally important, and he has developed the hypothesis that interactive effects exist between uncertainty and dependence. In other words, the worst situation for an organization is to be dependent and uncertain. A comprehensive theory of IOR will have to incorporate both views of the environment.

Our approach here will be to first review the theoretical models developed to explain the flow of resources and information between organizations in dyads. In particular, we will assess the influence of the resource exchange model as developed by Levine and White (1961) because of its importance in the literature. In recent years, however, the Levine and White model has been severely criticized. Challenges come mainly from those who emphasize the impact of relative power and dependence on dyadic interaction: from those who endorse a resource dependence model. Propositions representative of the resource exchange model and the resource dependence model will be developed and presented in this chapter. Data from a study of organizations that serve delinquent and predelinquent youth will be used to illustrate how dyadic variables can be developed and propositions about interaction in dyads evaluated.

Miller (1958) observed some time ago that conflict between organizations at the community level impeded the development and delivery of services for delinquency prevention and control. Reid (1964) has expressed concern about the lack of coordination, duplication of services, and conflict that occurs between organizations. Reid anticipated that planners would call for the development of coordinating agencies to help overcome these constraints. Coordinating agencies would be premature, he argued, until a great deal more had been learned about variables that affect the relationships between organizations. Reid (1975) has been optimistic that the theoretical model developed by Levine and White (1961) offered hope for those interested in learning more about when and why organizations interact.

Levine and White Model

In order to achieve their respective goals, organizations must have three main resources; namely, recipients to serve, resources, and the service of personnel to direct the resources to recipients. Organizations that lack needed resources may engage in exchanges with other organizations. Levine and White (1961, pp.

588–589) have defined exchange as any voluntary activity between two organizations that has consequences for their respective goals or objectives. In their analysis of community health and welfare organizations, Levine and White specified three determinants of exchange:

1. the lack of accessibility of organizations to necessary elements from outside the local system,

2. the objectives of each organization and particular functions to which it allocates the elements that it controls, and

3. the degree to which domain consensus exists among the various organizations.

Levine, White, and Paul (1963, pp. 1187–1194) have stated that the student of health and welfare organizations should try to determine the types of cooperation sought by organizations and from whom. In order to answer these questions, we must direct our attention away from the properties of particular organizations and focus upon comparative and relational properties when analyzing the behavior in dyads. Levine et al. make explicit reference to dyads when discussing the determinants of exchange. For example, in their disucssion of domain consensus (mutually agreed-upon conceptions of domains), they state that unless domains are clarified, competition may occur between two organizations. They state that two organizations may resolve conflict between them by specifying the criteria for the referral of patients to them. In their discussion of functions, they state that in general, agencies with little familiarity about each other's services do not interact much with each other. They observe, too, that a lack of cooperation between two agencies may be due to different degrees of professionalism. A similar implicit, and sometimes explicit, orientation toward, and appreciation of the importance of, dyadic interaction can also be found in the works of Litwak and Hylton (1962) and Guetzkow (1966).

Some debate does exist with regard to the meaning of key concepts in Levine and White's model, and some of these concepts have been reconceptualized to focus more specifically upon interorganizational concerns and to resolve the criticism that they are tautological. For example, Warren, Rose, and Bergunder (1974, pp. 19–27) have provided a useful elaboration of domain consensus, defining it as an organization's locus in the interorganizational field, including its manifest goals and its channels of access to task and maintenance resources. Cook (1977, p. 64) has stated that Levine and White's definition of exchange is so broad that it includes any form of voluntary activity between organizations, rendering the term synonymous with interaction. Following Cook, exchange in this analysis is taken to mean voluntary transactions involving the transfer of resources (including information) between two or more organizations.

Debate exists, too, about the form the proposition involves goals and functions and exchanges between organizations should take. Levine and White (1961) have pointed out that organizations that provide direct treatment to clients rate highest on number of client referrals and amount of resources received. But Levine and White do not indicate if organizations with similar or dissimilar goals are most likely to exchange. Reid (1964, p. 421) draws the conclusion that exchanges are most likely between organizations with similar goals because each organization has a stake in the goal attainment of the other. Although he had predicted the opposite, Paulson (1976, pp. 320–321) has found that perceived cooperation and perceived competition are positively related to goal similarity.

Research results with regard to the role of domain consensus and resource scarcity are mixed. Braito, Paulson, and Klonglan (1972) have called domain consensus a key interorganizational variable. Braito et al., in their study of single organizations and their exchanges, have found that domain consensus was significantly related to the age of the organization, the organization's formalization, resources allocated by the organization to the problem area, and number of board members. Adamek and Lavin (1975), in an analysis of the resource scarcity hypothesis, have found that organizations with the most resources more frequently engage in exchanges than organizations with fewer resources. Adamek and Lavin do not see these results as necessarily contradicting Levine and White. Adamek and Lavin suggest that it is resource scarcity at the collectivity level that may lead to exchanges, and they had focused upon single organizations in their study. Paulson (1976) has found that domain consensus and resource differences are positively related to perceived co-operation in dyads. Others whose research has been influenced by Levine and White's model include Guetzkow (1966), Molnar (1976), and Van de Ven (1980).

Levine and White's model also has been used in discussions of conflict between organizations, even though no specific propositions about conflict were made in their original formulation. Following Warren et al. (1974, p. 45), conflict is taken to mean interaction directed at achieving contrary issue outcomes. Reid (1964) has suggested that scarcity of resources, a lack of domain consensus, and goal similarity can lead to conflict. Molnar and Rogers (1979) have found that, when other variables are controlled, goal similarity is associated with conflict. Akinbode and Clark (1976), who have attempted to develop a general framework for analyzing IOR, have also specified propositions about conflict and exchange. Akinbode and Clark state that exchanges are a function of domain consensus, scarcity, and partial interdependence; conflict is thought to be a function of dissimilar goals, a lack of domain consensus, and ideological differences. This summary of the resource exchange model suggests the following propositions:

Resource exchanges will be positively correlated with:

1. scarcity of resources,

2. domain consensus,

3. lack of alternative resources, and

4. goal similarity.

Conflict will be negatively related to:

5. domain consensus;

but positively related to:

6. scarcity of resources,
7. lack of alternative resources, and
8. goal similarity.

Resource Dependence Model

Expansions of Levine and White's basic model, and challenges to it, are increasingly seen in the literature (e.g., Aldrich, 1976; Benson, 1975; Cook, 1977; Hall, Clark, Grondano, Johnson and Van Roekel, 1977; Paulson, 1976; Schmidt and Kochan, 1977; Van de Ven, 1980). Aldrich (1979, pp. 265–273) provides an excellent summary of the key elements of the resource dependence model that constitutes the principal challenge to Levine and White's model. Avoiding or exploiting dependence relations is a central dynamic of IOR, and concepts of dependence and relative power are crucial to interorganizational analysis. Aldrich states that Levine and White's definition of voluntary exchange captures the "normal" aspect of exchanges brought about in the absence of power differences and dependencies. Some dependencies are sought, however, (or avoided) because of power differences and the control possibilities inherent in the state of dependence. Organizations that acquire a monopoly over resources are able to establish dependencies over other organizations that cannot reciprocate resource exchanges. Blau (1964, p. 118) has specified the conditions that must be present for the possession of resources to lead to power:

1. an organization does not have resources to reciprocate,
2. no alternative suppliers exist,
3. no possibilities exist for using coercive power against the resource holder, and
4. the organization cannot get along without the scarce resources.

Dependence, as formulated by Emerson (1962, p. 32), exists to the degree that one actor has a motivational investment in goals mediated by another actor and inversely to the degree that the goals are available outside the relationship. Aldrich thinks that Emerson's concept of dependence incorporates Levine and White's (1961) concept of exchange in all but one aspect, the concept of domain consensus. Aldrich hypothesizes that domain consensus does not cause exchanges but only results because of exchanges or is developed to justify exchanges (Aldrich, 1979, p. 269).

Schellenberg (1965), in one of the few empirical studies of dependence, has found that the perceived value, or motivational investment aspect of dependence, may be more crucial than the value of alternatives aspect. Jacobs (1974) has related the concept of "essentiality" to the potential variability and flexibility an organization has in responding to dependence. Essentiality is a function of the degree to which an organization's goals, technology, and activity system are influenced by environment pressures. Schmidt and Kochan (1977), who have conducted an empirical study of symmetrical and asymmetrical relations, conceptualize dependence as the motivation to interact with another organization. The emphasis taken here will be to stress the perceived value of the relationship when dependence is discussed and measured.

We are cautioned not to overstate the importance of asymmetric dependencies because they may not be stable over time. Aldrich (1979, pp. 269–274) states that asymmetric dependence is usually not present in most transactions. Why is this the case? When asymmetric dependencies exist, the least dependent organizations may seek information that will enable them to maintain their positions. But exchanges between organizations may proliferate to wider circles as the more dependent organizations seek to establish symmetric (mutual) dependence relations with other organizations to decrease their dependence on dominant organizations (Blau, 1964, pp. 190–194).

Cook (1977, pp. 67–68) discusses situations, too, in which asymmetric dependencies will decrease over time if more powerful organizations actually use their power advantage to increase the rewards they receive. The use of a power advantage to acquire increased levels of resources from a single source actually leads to an increased dependence upon the relation over time. Benson (1975, pp. 235–236) and Blalock and Wilken (1979, p. 552) also suggest that networks tend toward balance, and Pfeffer and No-wak (1976), in their research with business firms, have found that resource scarcity and mutual dependencies lead to joint business ventures. The conclusion reached after this review of literature and research is that mutual dependence, more than asymmetric dependence, will be positively correlated with exchanges.

Concern has been shown for variables that can operate to increase administrators' awareness of dependencies and therefore increase the likelihood of exchanges between organizations. It has been observed that mutual dependencies and exchanges often are accompanied by high rates of interaction (Blalock and Wilken, 1979; Litwak and Hylton, 1962; Schmidt and Kochan, 1977). Aldrich (1979, p. 424) adds that administrators also seek a high rate of interaction to promote exchanges and to make visible the consequences of their organizations' efforts. There-fore, it should be expected that frequency of interaction will be positively correlated with exchanges. Hall et al. (1977), in their analysis of organizations that serve problem youth, state that one of the most interesting findings for them was that the frequency of interaction was significantly related to both coordination and conflict. Contact between organizations is necessary for conflict to occur, and the more frequently interaction occurs, the more likely is the conflict. In addition, conflict, once it has developed, may require interaction for its resolution. For these reasons, fre-quency of interaction is hypothesized to be positively correlated with conflict.

We already have seen that Levine and White's determinants of exchange included a consideration of organizations' goals and functions and their resource base. It has been proposed that or-ganizational similarity will be positively correlated with ex-changes. Administrators from organizations that are similar may find it easier to relate to each other and be less likely to have conflict. Which additional comparative properties should be considered? Obviously, many are possible. Because human service organizations are labor intensive, properties that are most likely to influence the interaction between personnel in and outside their own organizations should be given preference for consideration. Differences in social status and professionalism have been discussed in terms of producing interpersonal imbalances between personnel from different organizations (Haas and Drabek, 1973, p. 244) and professional status subordination (Kriesberg, 1973), and it is thought that these differences may hinder exchanges and make conflict more likely.

To date, very little research on comparative properties has been done at the dyad level and the actual empirical results are mixed. Paulson (1976) has found that differences, measured in terms of administrators' education and salary, are negatively associated with perceived cooperation. Molnar (1976) has found that a set of decision-maker variables, including education and professional activity in associations, was not significantly related to exchanges nor to domain consensus. Nevertheless, zero-order correlations reported by Molnar (1976, pp. 178–179) between differences in education and exchanges were negative and significant.

Aiken and Hage (1968) have specified that organizations that are more formal are more likely to develop exchange relations. But what about the role of comparative formalization? Organizations that are different in formalization may be less likely to engage in exchanges. This is because organizational personnel may find it difficult to relate to each other, and conflict may result. Molnar (1976, p. 179) found that zero-order correlations between differences in formalization and exchanges are not significant for agencies concerned with managing natural resources. Comparative formalization may be more crucial, however, for some kinds of organizations such as human service organizations. In sum, the weight of the literature and limited empirical research suggests that differences in organizational properties will be positively correlated with conflict and negatively correlated with exchanges.

Although much more empirical research has focused upon resource exchanges than upon conflict, the role of conflict in IOR is receiving increasing attention. After their review of existing theory and empirical research, Molnar and Rogers (1979, p. 407) conclude that the net effect of interdependencies, including resource exchanges, upon conflict is thought to be positive. Their research supports this view. Others who have discussed the high probability of exchanges leading to conflict between organizations include Miller (1958), Barth (1963), Aiken and Hage (1968), Pfeffer and Salancik (1978), and Mulford and Mulford (1977).

The approach taken in the research with organizations that serve youth reported here will be to add the additional propositions suggested by resource dependence advocates to those specified for the Levine and White model. We will evaluate the usefulness of the Levine and White propositions alone versus the Levine and White propositions plus others that have been developed by resource dependence advocates for explaining resource exchanges and conflict. In addition to those propositions already discussed above, these propositions are suggested by the resource dependence literature:

Resource exchange will be positively correlated with:

9. perceived mutual dependence and
10. frequency of interaction;

and negatively correlated with:

11. differences in organizational properties.

Conflict will be positively correlated with:

12. perceived mutual dependence,
13. frequency of interaction,
14. dissimilar organizational properties, and
15. resource exchanges.

In summary, we have reviewed the two major theoretical models of resource exchanges and have specified some of the relevant propositions. The relatively few empirical studies of dyadic relations have acted as a barrier to the assimilation of knowledge. More dyadic studies are needed and some of these should be longitudinal in design. Given the fact that relatively few studies have been completed, all existing data sets should be sought out and used. In the section that follows, data are reported from a recent study with human service organizations in one community. Keeping in mind the study limitations, let's use these data to learn all that we can about dyadic relations.

RESEARCH SETTING AND METHODS

The organizations studied in this midwestern community[1] are concerned with services for delinquent and predelinquent youth, and constitute what Aldrich (1979:280) calls an "action set." Some of the organizations have a county-wide responsibility, but the focus here is on the interaction among these core organizations that provide services, or funding for services, in this community and one small community nearby. Utilizing methods consistent with those discussed by Aldrich (1974) and Warren et al. (1974), core organizations were selected and interviews conducted with the chief administrator of each organization and/or with the person named by the administrator as the one who interacted most with the other core organizations.

The 17 core organizations[2] included a group shelter house, a county probation office, judicial magistrate court, police department, county social services, county attorney's office, county board of supervisors, a church group home, a local mental health center, an alcoholism regional center, a community action agency, a senior high school, two junior high schools, a school system in a small community nearby, a community office of the state employment service, and the city council. Data were obtained about each organization and its interactions with the other 16 core organizations that provided services for delinquent or predelinquent youth. The dyad is the unit of analysis in this research, and a total of 136 dyads are analyzed.[3]

Dependent Variables

Multiple indicators[4] for resource exchange and conflict were used. Please refer to the last section of this chapter for detailed notes with regard to the measurement of all concepts.

Resource Exchanges (Y_1-Y_5). A number of authors have identified information exchange, resource exchange, joint programs, formal agreements, and the exchange of board members as relevant dimensions of exchange (Aiken and Hage, 1968; Marrett, 1971; Pfeffer, 1973; Rogers, 1974). Five dimensions of exchange were used in this study.

Y_1:   Information Exchange. In index composed of three items: (1) personal acquaintance with administrators in other organizations, (2) recent meetings with other administrators to discuss organizational activities, and (3) inclusion of organizations on mailing lists.

Y_2:   Resource Exchange. A single item asking about the extent to which other organizations have provided needed resources.

Y_3:   Joint Activities. A single item asking about working with other organizations in jointly planning and programming services.

Y_4:   Written Agreements. A single item asking about the existence of written agreements with other organizations.

Y_5:   Board Members. A single item asking if organizations had placed organizational members on boards or committees of other organizations.

Conflict (Y_6-Y_7). Conflict was measured by two variables, the compatibility of operating philosophies and operating conflict. See Paulson (1976), Hall et al. (1977), and Molnar and Rogers (1979) for a variety of ways that conflict has been measured.

Y_6:   Compatibility of Operating Philosophy. A single item asking about the extent to which operating philosophies were perceived as compatible.

Y_7:   Operating Conflict. A single item asking the extent to which disputes characterize relationships.

Independent Variables

Levine and White Determinants (X_1-X_4). Resource scarcity and the three determinants were operationalized following suggestions provided by Paulson (1976), Hall et al. (1977), and Molnar (1978).

X_1: Resource Scarcity. An index composed of three items; namely, scarcity of: (1) physical facilities, (2) number of paid personnel, and (3) number of volunteers.

X_2: Domain Consensus. A single item used to ask respondents the degree to which they thought other organizations should be included in new programs.

X_3: Lack of Alternative Sources of Resources. A single item asking the degree to which most of the organization's funds come from local sources or from alternative sources at state or federal levels.

X_4: Goal Similarity. Degree to which major services provided by organizations are similar.

Key Resource Dependence Variables (X_5-X_{10}). Guidelines for the development of these variables are provided by Paulson (1976), Rogers, (1974), and Hall et al. (1977).

X_5: Mutual Dependence. Degree to which contacts with other organizations are seen as important for the work of the organization.

X_6: Asymmetric Dependence. Difference in degree to which contacts with other organizations are seen as important for the work of the organizations.

X_7: Frequency of Interaction. Frequency with which agencies have contacts with each other, varying from a few times a year to one or more times a day.

Variables X_8-X_{10}: were developed consistent with the guidelines by Paulson (1976), Hall et al. (1977), and Molnar (1978).

X_8: Difference in Professionalism. Difference in educational level of majority of paid workers.

X_9: Difference in Degree of Social Status. Difference in average salary paid to workers.

X_{10}: Differences in Formalization. Difference in degree to which referrals are made to written policies.

Results

It has been pointed out that debate exists about whether or not Levine and White's model of resource exchange is relevant for explaining relationships that result in part because of mandates (Cook, 1977; Hall et al., 1977). Respondents were asked to indicate the primary basis of the relationship between their organization and each of the 16 other organizations. In only 19 of 136 dyads did respondents indicate that their relationship was required by law. Respondents most frequently stated that the primary basis of the contact was common practice or because of a specific need or problem. As we shall see later in this section, formal agreements were fairly common. But because the dyadic interaction resulted from mandates in only a small percentage of the cases, the study does serve as a suitable setting for discussion of Levine and White's model and the resource dependency model.

Pearson correlation coefficients are presented in Tables 4-1 and 4-2. These correlations are used to analyze the relationships

Table 4-1. Zero-Order Coefficients of Correlations Between Exchange and Conflict

Exchange and Conflict Variables	Y_1	Y_2	Y_3	Y_4	Y_5	Y_6	Y_7
Information Exchange Y_1	X						
Resource Exchange Y_2	.321*	X					
Joint Activities Y_3	.630*	.369*	X				
Formal Agreements Y_4	.558*	.495*	.470*	X			
Board Members Y_5	.394*	.093	.211*	.256*	X		
Compatible Philsophies Y_6	.208*	.142	.186*	.202*	.137	X	
Operating Conflict Y_7	.185*	.067	.297*	.158*	−.020	−.485*	X

* = Significant at the .05 level. N for analysis varies from 125 to 136 because of missing data.

Table 4-2. Zero-Order Coefficients of Correlation Between Dependent and Independent Variables

Independent Variables:	Dependent Variables:						
	Information Exchange Y_1	Resource Exchange Y_2	Joint Activities Y_3	Formal Agreements Y_4	Board Members Y_5	Compatible Philosophies Y_6	Operating Conflict Y_7
Resource Scarcity X_1	.170*	.190*	.265*	.213*	.169*	.053	.192*
Domain Consensus X_2	.250*	.034	.210*	.167*	.072	.145	.131
Lack of Alternatives X_3	-.137	-.054	-.160*	-.087	-.136	-.135	-.051
Goal Similarity X_4	.158*	.032	.062	.138	.097	.230*	.032
Mutual Dependence X_5	.478*	.235*	.533*	.353*	.146*	.243*	.202*
Asymmetric Dependence X_6	-.230*	-.011	-.106	-.163*	-.093	-.100	-.040

Frequency of Interactions X_7	.515*	.229*	.465*	.425*	.248*	.090	.386*
Difference in Professionalism X_8	.019	.094	-.075	.114	-.093	-.037	.020
Difference in Social Status X_9	-.126	-.232*	-.100	-.046	-.147*	.093	-.115
Difference in Formalization X_{10}	.006	-.047	.129	.054	-.118	-.186*	.203*
Multiple R =	.576	.413	.594	.562	.377	.475	.511
	(.241)	(.200)	(.297)	(.341)	(.194)	(.286)	(.219)
Multiple R^2 =	.333	.171	.352	.315	.142	.225	.261
	(.058)	(.040)	(.088)	(.117)	(.038)	(.082)	(.048)

* = Significant at the .05 level. N for analysis varies from 125 to 136 because of missing data.

between the variables used as measures of resource exchange and conflict and to evaluate the propositions that are representative of Levine and White's resource exchange model and the resource dependency model. The correlation coefficients provide evidence of the association between any two variables. Correlation coefficients tell us about the extent to which two variables are associated with each other. Correlations can vary from 1.000 to -1.000. A positive correlation coefficient indicates that, as one variable increases, the second variable increases too. A negative correlation indicates that, as one variable increases, the second variable decreases. An asterisk (*) has been placed in Tables 4-1 and 4-2 by each correlation that is so strong that it is unlikely to be due to chance more than five times out of one hundred.

An analysis of the correlation results presented in Table 4-1 indicates that they are nearly all significant and positive. This means that the more likely one kind of exchange occurs in dyads, the more likely other kinds of exchanges also occur. Rogers (1974) has discussed the advantages of a single overall measure of exchange and has found some evidence that a reliable measure can be developed for the analysis of particular organizations. The data presented herein, however, are at the dyad level, and at least one variable (Y_5) correlates poorly with other measures of exchange. This suggests that the exchange of board members may function primarily as an aid to information exchanges but not to resource exchanges.

As we might expect, the variable indicative of compatible philosophies in dyads (Y_6) is significantly and negatively correlated with operating conflict. The results in Table 4-1 indicate that exchanges of resources and information are more likely when compatible philosophies exist. It is also apparent that exchanges may sometimes lead to operating conflict, with joint activities being the exchange variable most highly correlated with operating conflict.

Propositions 1 to 4 state that measures of resource exchange will be positively correlated with scarcity of resources, domain consensus, lack of alternative sources of resources, and goal similarity. Propositions 5 to 8 state that conflict will be related negatively to domain consensus but positively with scarcity, lack of alternative sources of resources, and goal similarity. From Table 4-2, one can see that domain consensus is significantly correlated with information exchange, joint activities, and formal agreements, as predicted, but not with resource exchange, the exchange of board members, or with conflict. Note that the correlations involving domain consensus (positive evaulations of each other's domain) are generally weak, which means that domain consensus is not associated with exchanges or conflict to the degree predicted by the resource exchange model.

Resource scarcity is significantly correlated with all measures of resource exchange and operating conflict. Lack of resource alternatives is significantly (but negatively) correlated only with joint activities. Goal similarity is significantly correlated with information exchange and with compatible philosophy. The general conclusion reached is that the variables used to represent the Levine and White model are poorly correlated with resource exchanges and conflict, except for resource scarcity. And the correlations involving resource scarcity are generally modest.

Propositions 9 to 15 are thought to be representative of the expansion and modification of the Levine and White model to the resource dependence model. The propositions state that mutual dependence, frequency of interaction, and similar organizational properties will be correlated positively with exchanges and negatively with conflict. In addition, resource exchange variables (Y_1-Y_5) are hypothesized to be positively correlated with conflict. Mutual dependence, and not asymmetric dependence, is significantly correlated with each of the dependent variables. Frequency of interaction is significantly correlated with each measure of exchange and with operating conflict. Differences in professionalism and differences in social status are poorly correlated with the dependent variables. Differences in formalization are correlated negatively with compatible philosophy and positively with operating conflict. The conclusion reached on the basis of these correlations is that resource scarcity, mutual dependence—but not asymmetric dependence—and frequency of interaction seem to be relatively crucial variables.

Resource scarcity, mutual dependence, and frequency of interaction are involved in more significant correlations that any other set of independent variables. These results are consistent with Van de Ven (1980, p. 336) who found, in his study of 14 early childhood development organizations and 133 other agencies during 1974, that mutual dependence and frequency of communication were significantly associated with all measures of resource exchanges in dyads. Asymmetric dependence is significantly and negatively correlated with information exchange and with formal agreements. In general, asymmetric dependence is but poorly correlated with the variables. This means that balanced relationships are more crucial than unbalanced ones for this set of organizations.

The multiple correlation coefficients (R) and coefficients of determination (R^2) are reported to evaluate the overall power of the models to account for variance in the dependent variables. The coefficient of determination (R^2) indicates the percent of variance in the dependent variable that is jointly explained by the independent variables in the model.

The R and R^2 values are presented at the bottom of Table 4-2. The R and R^2 values presented in parentheses are for the first four independent variables: for resource scarcity and for measures of the three "determinants" of exchanges specified by Levine and White. It should be observed that the R^2 values associated with the Levine and White model are generally low, with the largest being .117 for formal agreements. This means that the variables associated with the Levine and White model jointly explain only a small percent of the variance in the dependent variables.

The R and R^2 values for the overall model are considerably higher than those for the Levine and White model alone. These results indicate that the expanded model has considerably more power for explaining variance that the Levine and White model.

Regular multiple regression is a statistical procedure for identifying the independent variables that as a group are most powerful for explaining variance in dependent variables. The results of the regular multiple regression analysis indicate that resource scarcity, mutual dependence, and frequency of interaction are the three most powerful independent variables for explaining variance in the five exchange variables. The group of independent variables most associated with compatible philosophies includes goal similarity, mutual dependence, and difference in formalization—with comparable formalization being associated positively with compatible philosophies. The group of variables most associated with operating conflict includes resource scarcity, frequency of interaction, and difference in formalization.

SUMMARY

These results are positive from the point of view of theory and research. At least a modest amount of variance is jointly accounted for by the variables in the models. Measurement problems in general, the need for longitudinal research, and the field expense involved in studying sets of organizations are among the major problems constraining research on dyads and larger units. More severe, though, are theoretical constraints. Because most of the variance in dependent variables has not been accounted for, it may be necessary to add additional concepts to our models. One of the greatest challenges that remains is to develop logically related sets of propositions, perhaps with path analysis and causal model approaches, for explaining dyadic interaction. More attention should be given to specifying the relevant concepts for theory at the dyad level. Greater care should be given to determining which comparative organizational properties are relevant and how they operate. In addition, the impact of near and remote environmental dimensions must be considered.

Caution must be observed when attempting to generalize from these results. The set of organizations studied was small and may be different from other sets. Suggestions made in the past about how the likelihood of exchanges can be increased do seem to be supported here. More frequent interaction, promoting perceived mutual dependencies, and the possibility of obtaining scarce resources may encourage exchanges. Organizations that experience scarcity are more likely to conflict, especially if they are different in structure and in frequent contact with each other. Operating conflict is significantly and positively correlated with information exchange, joint activites, and formal agreements in this study. This means that interdependencies may be a major source of operating conflict. Conflict, then, cannot always be avoided, and probably coexists with exchanges in dyads. Practitioners probably are more likely than other specialists to understand the positive and negative consequences of both conflict and exchanges for the delivery of services for youth. Their intuitive and grounded perspectives on causes of conflict and exchanges also are valuable. Team research, involving theory and methods specialists, and practitioners, holds promise for the future.

Three additional points should be observed at this time. The dyadic research reported in this chapter does tell us a considerable amount about the organizations and agencies in this action set that serve predelinquent and delinquent youth. But further research involving other kinds of organizations is greatly needed. Are the same factors involved in conflict and exchanges between business organizations as between human service organizations? If not, what unique characteristics differentiate public and private sector interaction?

We know from Chapter 3 that some limited empirical research does exist to support the idea that the development of IOR does contribute to the effectiveness of particular organizations. Final questions to be asked here are: Are the joint activities of dyads "effective?" What factors contribute to the effectiveness of joint ventures? Unfortunately, almost no studies have been conducted in which the effectiveness of joint projects relative to projects by particular organizations have been compared. Van de Ven's (1980) study is one of the few that has examined factors associated with the effectiveness of relationships. Van de Ven found that perceived effectiveness was most highly correlated with mutual dependence, awareness of other organizations, communication, and resource exchanges. In addition, domain consensus was nearly as highly correlated with perceived effectiveness. Very high priority should be placed on studies in which the effectiveness of joint efforts are determined.

An analysis of dyadic interaction cannot tell us everything about an action set or a larger collectivity. The emergence, persistence, and demise of interorganizational collectivities (ICs) may be caused, or at least influenced, by general environmental conditions, by comprehensive system properties, or by mandates from higher levels. These issues and others will be considered in Chapter 6 when we turn to an in-depth analysis of larger collectivities. Another issue has to do with boundary spanners, those people who represent and negotiate for their organizations. Increasingly, the importance of boundary spanners is being recognized, and models are being developed to analyze constraints on the role performance of boundary spanners. These important considerations will be taken up next.

DISCUSSION QUESTIONS

1. What is dyadic analysis? What is its importance?

2. What are comparative properties and why are they required for analyzing dyadic interaction?

3. According to Levine and White, what are the three "determinants" of resource exchanges?

4. How does the resource dependence model differ conceptually from Levine and White's model?

5. Can you think of examples of symmetric and asymmetric dependencies in your community? Which kind of dependencies predominate?

6. Which of the factors thought to be related to the frequency of resource exchanges could most easily be influenced by third parties?

7. Why might it be expected that resource exchanges will sometimes lead to conflict between organizations?

8. Which correlation results reported in this chapter will be of most interest to practitioners such as those interested in community development or in the delivery of services?

9. In addition to human service organizations, to
   what degree are the results reported here applicable to other kinds of organizations? Why?

10. Why is longitudinal research on dyadic relations
    needed?

A FICTITIOUS CASE STUDY: THE RELUCTANT PARTNERS

Events were precipitated by the death of a teenage boy from
a drug overdose. Many residents had not really believed that
youth-related problems existed in Glenton. The teenage boy's
death presented a crisis that could not be denied. Parents, teachers, and community leaders resolved that this should not happen
again and that some sort of community education program
should be developed to help young people with drug or related
problems. It was soon evident that no single organization could
solve the problem or do all of the work that was needed.

Tom Edwards, the mayor of Glenton, has taken the lead in
sounding out citizens to find out which organizations should be
involved in the community effort and in proposing ways to work
together. Based upon his preliminary work, Tom Edwards has
determined that the core organizations for the education effort
should include the two junior and one senior high schools, the
local community hospital, police, mental health center, county
social services, and juvenile probation. Each of these organizations is important because each already has relevant programs
for youth, regular contacts with youth, or the resources required
for such programs. Tom Edwards was able to get a verbal commitment from leaders in these organizations, and each organization assigned a person to serve on Glenton's Drug Education
committee.

Unfortunately, nothing has really been accomplished in
Glenton. Regular meetings of the committee are still held, but
the attendance has been poor. Several kinds of disagreements
and conflict have developed during recent weeks. Tom Jakes,
police representative, missed several meetings, and during the
last meeting was quite negative about ideas expressed by others.
He dislikes the "education" aspect of the committee and said

openly that it should be a drug "enforcement" effort. Jakes said that "education has already failed—and this is at least partly due to the way schools are run by the kids these days." Leslie Rogers, the high school principal, serves on the committee and thinks that many youth disrespect the local police. Rogers wonders if the police should even be involved in the committee work. Betty Wilson, a youth probation worker, tried to get Rogers and Jakes to see each other's point of view but has not really succeeded. Wilson thinks that the committees' work is doomed unless the others can get the police and schools to work together.

Complaints also developed because one committee member, from the county social services, seemed unwilling to really get involved or commit his organization. John Blake, the newly appointed director of county social services, stated during the last committee meeting that his agency's budget for the year was already set and that no funds could be assigned to any drug education program in the near future. This surprised the others present at the meeting because no funds or personnel have been requested at this time from any organizations. Charles Voss, the administrator of the local hospital, thinks that more frequent committee meetings should be held. He has suggested that the committee members do not really know much about each others' work that relates to youth. Following Voss' suggestion, each committee member took time during the next several meetings to briefly describe his/her organization's work, and it has been suggested that meetings should be hosted by the different committee members in a room available to their organization.

QUESTIONS FOR CASE ANALYSIS

1. If you were called upon to act as a facilitator for this committee, what would you do?

2. What are the major problems? Do you think that relations between the police and schools can be improved?

3. Would the complete resolution of conflict be your goal, why or why not?

MEASUREMENT OF VARIABLES

Dyadic Variables	*Item(s) and Code*
Y_1 Information Exchange	1. "Are you acquainted with the director in charge of _____ ?"
	2. "Have you met with the director of _____ at any time during the past year to discuss the activities of your respective organizations?"
	3. "Is _____ on your organization's mailing list to receive newsletters, annual reports, and other information releases?"
	Each item was coded 1 for No and 2 for Yes. The three items were first summed for each organization; then, the totals were summed for organizations in each dyad.
Y_2 Resource Exchange	"How would you describe the extent to which _____ provides needed resources such as meeting rooms, personnel, equipment, or funds to your organization as you try to accomplish your objectives?"
	Coded 1–5 with 1 being Low and 5 High. Scores were summed for the two organizations in each dyad.

Dyadic Variables	*Item(s) and Code*
Y_3 Joint Activities	"Within the last three years, has your organization worked jointly in planning and implementing any specific services or activity with _____ ?" Coded 1 for No and 2 for Yes. Scores were summed for each dyad.
Y_4 Formal Agreements	"Does your organization have any written agreements with _____ pertaining to specific programs or activities, personnel commitments, client referrals, procedures for working together, or for an activity?" Coded 1 for No and 2 for Yes. Scores were summed for each dyad.
Y_5 Board Members	"Does anyone from ____serve on boards, councils, or committees of your organization?" Coded 1 for No and 2 for Yes. Scores were summed for each dyad.
Y_6 Compatible Philosophy	"How compatible is your organization's operating philosophy with _____ ?" Coded 1–5 with 1 being Low and 5 High. Scores were summed for each dyad.

Dyadic Variables	*Item(s) and Code*
Y_7 Operating Conflict	"To what extent do disagreements or disputes characterize the relationship between your organization and ____ ?" Coded 1–5 with 1 being Low and 5 High. Scores were summed for each dyad.
X_1 Resource Scarcity	1. "Adequacy of physical facilities?" 2. "Adequacy of number of paid personnel (professionals)?" 3. "Adequacy of number of volunteers? Each item coded 1–3 with 1 being More Than Enough, 2—Enough, and 3—Fewer Than Enough. The three items were first summed for each organization; then, the totals were summed for organizations in each dyad.
X_2 Domain Consensus	"If a new interorganizational program designed to work with the juvenile offender were to be started in this county, do you think ____ should be involved in it?" Coded 1 for No and 2 for Yes. Scores were summed for each dyad.
X_3 Lack of Alternative Sources of Funds	"What is your primary source of funds?"

Dyadic Variables	*Item(s) and Code*
X_3 (Cont.)	Coded 1 for Federal, 2—State, 3—County, 4—City, and 5—for Organizational Campaign in Local Areas. Scores were summed for organizations in each dyad. The higher the score, the more funds are secured at the local level and the less alternatives are available.
X_4 Goal Similarity	"What is the major service provided directly by your organization?"
	Dyads with organizations having similar services were coded 1 and those with dissimilar services a 0.
X_5 Perceived Mutual Dependence	"How important are the contacts with _____ to the work of your organization?
	Coded 1–5 with 1 being Low and 5 High. Scores were summed for each dyad.
X_6 Asymmetric Dependence	Refer above to question used to build X_5. Scores were developed for each dyad by obtaining the difference to the responses given by organizations for each dyad.
X_7 Frequency of Interaction	"How often does your organization have contact with each of these organizations?"

Coded 1 for A Few Times A Year, 2—About Once A Month, 3—About Once A Week, 4—A Couple Of Times A Week, and 5—One or More Times a Day. Scores were summed for each dyad.

X_8 Differences in Professionalism

"Educational level of majority of paid workers (professionals)?"

Coded 1 for High School, 2—High School And Some College, or High School And Special Training Other Than College, 3—College, and 4—Education Beyond College Graduate. Differences were obtained between the scores for organizations in each dyad.

X_9 Differences in Social Status

"Paid salary of majority of paid workers (professionals)?"

Coded 1 for Less Than $10,000, 2—$10,000 To $14,000, 3—$14,000 to $18,000, and 4 —$18,000 Plus. Differences were obtained between the scores for organizations in each dyad.

X_{10} Differences in Formalization

"Frequency of referral to written policies by your organization?"

Coded 1 for Never, 2—Oc-
casionally, 3—Usually, and
4—Always. Differences were
obtained between the scores
for organizations in each
dyad.

REFERENCES

Adamek, R. J., & Lavin, B. F. Interorganizational exchange: A note on the scarcity hypothesis. In A. R. Negandi (Ed.), *Interorganizational theory.* Kent, OH: Kent State University Press, 1975, pp. 196–210.

Aiken, M., & Hage., J., Organizational interdependence and intraorganizational structure. *American Sociological Review,* 1968, *33,* 912–930.

Akinbode, I. A., & Clark, R. C. A framework for analyzing interorganizational relationships. *Human Relations,* 1976, *29,* 101–114.

Aldrich, H. E. *The environment as a network of organizations: Theoretical and methodological implications.* Prepared for Research Committee on Organizations Section of International Sociological Association Meetings, Toronto, Canada, August, 1974.

————Resource dependence and interorganizational relations. *Administration and Society,* 1976, *7,* 419–453.

————*Organizations and environments.* Englewood Cliffs, NJ: Prentice-Hall, 1979.

Aldrich, H. E., & Pfeffer, J. Environments of organizations. In A. Inkeles (Ed.), *Annual review of sociology, Vol. II.* Palo Alto, CA: Annual Review, Inc., 1976, pp. 79–105.

Barth, E. A. T. The causes and consequences of interagency conflict. *Sociological Inquiry,* 1963, *33,* 51–55.

Benson, J. K. The interorganizational network as a political economy. *Administrative Science Quarterly,* 1975, *20,* 229–249.

Blalock, H. M., & Wilken, P. H. *Intergroup processes.* New York: The Free Press, 1979.

Blau, P. M. *Exchange and power in social life.* New York: John Wiley and Sons, 1964.

Braito, R., Paulson, S., & Klonglan, G. E. Domain consensus: A key variable in interorganizational analysis. In M. B. Brinkenhoff and P. R. Kuny, (Eds.), *Complex organizations and their environments.* Dubuque, IA: Wm. C. Brown Co., 1972, pp. 176–192.

Cook, K. S. Exchange and power in networks of interorganizational relations. *Sociological Quarterly,* 1977, *18,* 62–82.

Dill, W. R. Environment as an influence on managerial autonomy. *Administrative Science Quarterly,* 1958, *2,* 409–443.

Duncan, R. B. Characteristics of organizational environments and perceived environmental uncertainty. *Administrative Science Quarterly,* 1972, *17,* 313–327.

Emerson, R. M. Power-dependence relations. *American Sociological Review,* 1962, *27,* 31–40.

Guetzkow, H. Relations among organizations. In R. Bowers (Ed.), *Studies on behavior in organizations.* Athens, GA: University of Georgia Press, 1966, pp. 13–44.

Haas, J. E., & Drabek, T. *Complex organizations.* New York: Macmillan, 1973.

Hall, R. H., Clark, J. P., Grondano, P. C., Johnson, P. V., & Van Roekel, M. Patterns of interorganizational relationships. *Administrative Science Quarterly,* 1977, *22,* 437–474.

Jacobs, D. Dependency and vulnerability: An exchange approach to the control of organizations. *Administrative Science Quarterly,* 1974, *19,* 45–49.

Klonglan, G. E., Warren, R. D., Winkelpleck, J. M., & Paulson, S. K. Interorganizational measurement in the social services sector: Differences by hierarchical level. *Administrative Science Quarterly,* 1976, *21,* 675–687.

Kriesberg, L. Organizations and interpersonal cooperation. In W. V. Heydebrand (Ed.), *Comparative organizations.* Englewood Cliffs, NJ: Prentice-Hall, 1973, pp. 242–268.

Levine, S., & White, P. E. Exchange as a conceptual framework for the study of interorganizational relations. *Administrative Science Quarterly,* 1961, *5,* 583–601.

Levine, S., White, P. E. & Paul, B. D. Community interorganizational problems in providing medical care and social services. *American Journal of Public Health*, 1963, *58*, 1183–1195.

Litwak, E., & Hylton, L. Interorganizational analysis: A hypothesis on coordination. *Administrative Science Quarterly*, 1962, *6*, 395–420.

Marrett, C. B. On the specifications of interorganizational dimensions. *Sociology and Social Research*, 1971, *61*, 83–89.

Miller, W. B. Inter-institutional conflict as a major impediment to delinquency prevention. *Human Organization*, 1958, *17*, 20–23.

Molnar, J. J. The integration of interorganizational networks: Domain consensus and interdependence in organizational dyads. Unpublished Ph.D. dissertation, Iowa State University, Ames, IA, 1976.

————Comparative organizational properties and interorganizational interdependence. *Sociology and Social Research*, 1978, *63*, 24–48.

Molnar, J. J., & Rogers D. L. A comparative model of interorganizational conflict. *Administrative Science Quarterly* 1979, *24*, 406–423.

Mulford, C. L., & Mulford, M. A. Community and interorganizational perspectives on conflict and cooperation. *Rural Sociology*, 1977,*42*, 569–589.

Mulford, C. L., & Zober, E. Dyadic properties as correlates of exchange and conflict between organizations. Journal Paper No. J-10079 of the Iowa Agriculture and Home Economics Experiment Station, Sociology Department, Iowa State University, 1981, Ames, IA, Project No. 2271.

Paulson, S. K. A theory and comparative analysis of interorganizational dyads. *Rural Sociology*, 1976, *41*, 311–329.

Pennings, J. M. The relevance of the structural-contingency model for organizational effectiveness. *Administrative Science Quarterly*, 1975, *20*, 393–410.

Pfeffer, J. Size, composition, and function of hospital boards of directors: A study of environmental linkage. *Administrative Science Quarterly*, 1973, *18*, 349–363.

Pfeffer, J., & Nowak, P. Joint ventures and interorganizational dependence. *Administrative Science Quarterly*, 1976, *21*, 398–418.

Pfeffer, J., & Salancik, G. R. *The external control of organizations.* New York: Harper and Row, 1978.

Reid, W. Interagency coordination in delinquency prevention and control. *Social Science Review,* 1964, *38,* 418–428.

———Inter-organizational coordination in social welfare: A theoretical approach to analysis and intervention. In R. Kramer & H. Specht (Eds.), *Readings in community organization practice.* Englewood Cliffs, NJ: Prentice-Hall, 1975 pp. 176–187.

Rogers, D. L. Towards a scale of interorganizational relations among public agencies. *Sociology and Social Research,* 1974, *59,* 61–70.

Schellenberg, J. A. Dependence and cooperation. *Sociometry,* 1965, *28,* 158–172.

Schmidt, S. M., & Kochan, T. A. Interorganizational relationships: Patterns and motivations. *Administrative Science Quarterly,* 1977, *22,* 220–234.

Van de Ven, A. H. *Measuring and assessing organizations.* New York: John Wiley and Sons, 1980.

Warren, R. L., Rose, S. M., & Bergunder, A. F. *The structure of urban reform.* Lexington, MA: D. C. Heath and Company, 1974.

Weick, K. E. *The social phychology of organizing.* Reading, MA: Addison-Wesley, 1969.

NOTES

1. The research results from the study of the action network serving predelinquent and delinquent youth are adapted from Mulford and Zober (1981).

2. This research was conducted as part of an evaluation of the network by Medcor, Chicago during 1976. Zober developed the questionnaires used in this phase of the study, conducted the personal interviews, and her Ph.D. dissertation focused upon dyadic relationships. Mulford was an informal consusltant for this phase of the study, and worked with Zober in developing the questionnaires.

3. Some dyad scores were obtained by adding the scores for respondents; e.g., resource scarcity in the dyad X_1 and mutual de-

pendence X_5. Other dyad scores were obtained by determining the absolute difference in scores; e.g., difference in formalization X_{10} and difference in professionalism X_8. Finally, some dyad scores were obtained by coding the responses according to whether they were alike or different; e.g., goal similarity X_4.

4. Klonglan, Warren, Winkelpleck, and Paulson (1976), who developed the cumulative measures used by Rogers (1974), report that scaling difficulties were encountered when they attempted to develop a single scale across hierarchical levels. Their analysis produced three distinct item orderings, which correspond to the three hierarchical levels of state, district, and county. In sum, while the rationale for cumulative scales remains, there are still measurement difficulties.

Chapter 5

RELATIONS BETWEEN BOUNDARY SPANNERS

A close friend of mine who is the successful manager of a large department store seemed especially jubilant when we met for lunch recently. When I asked about the cause of his good feelings, he remarked that he had finally hired a person who showed promise as his "minister of foreign relations." He had hired a new personnel director! My friend pointed out that it was no easy task to find someone who could represent management in discussions with relevant state and federal agencies, participate in labor negotiations, and maintain the local store's personnel record system. My friend observed that one of the skills he looked for in other managers, too, was the ability to function effectively outside of the store—for example, at district meetings of corporation personnel, on buying trips when department managers select merchandise for upcoming seasons and negotiate wholesale costs and delivery times, and when the managers participate in local business organizations such as the chamber of commerce, Rotary, or Kiwanis.

I realized that universities, too, have their specialists in "foreign relations." Admissions directors must be able to work well with representatives of high schools. Some universities have "liaison personnel" who spend a great deal of time in our capitol interacting with agency personnel and negotiating research grants and contracts. Placement office personnel bring recruiters to campus and help schedule job interviews between company representatives and graduating students. Deans and other university officials leave the campus to brief state legislative committees and to confer and negotiate with their counterparts from other universities. Other examples that involve academic departments and services such as libraries, computer centers, residence halls, and purchasing services can be readily seen.

We have observed (see Chapters 3 and 4) that, for their survival, organizations must adapt to changes, obtain resources from their environment, and obtain information for decision making. What cannot be ignored is that this adaptation is largely aided through the behavior of individuals acting in boundary-spanning organizational positions. Nearly all organizations that receive inputs from, and discharge outputs to, other organizations in their environments develop specialized input and output roles for this purpose. Input and output roles, thus, are "boundary-spanning" roles because an organization is linked to its environment through interaction between members and nonmembers (Thompson, 1962).

In this chapter we will begin by looking at the ways that boundary-spanning roles differ from other organizational roles. For example, because of their unique nature, it has been suggested that persons who play boundary-spanning roles may be especially prone to role strain. Because boundary spanners are not as visible to management as other members, their control may be more problematic. We will examine some of the ways that organizations try to manage and control boundary spanners. In the third section we will focus upon factors that influence how boundary spanners from different organizations relate to each other. For example, what factors determine whether spanners will be cooperative and willing to bargain or negotiate or whether they will be antagonistic? Considerable empirical research has been conducted with boundary spanners during the

1970s; in the last section of this chapter we will review these results in order to evaluate the adequacy of existing models of boundary spanning.

BOUNDARY ROLES AND TRANSACTIONS WITH THE ENVIRONMENT

Thompson (1962) has observed that organizational output roles are defined in part by reciprocal roles of nonmembers. For example, roles for teachers, salesmen, and youth workers can only be understood in terms of students, customers, and clients. Although Thompson was primarily concerned with output roles, the same logic can be applied to input roles. Each input and output role, together with its reciprocating nonmember role, can be seen as a transaction structure. Parenthetically, boundary spanning also occurs between departments or subsystems within an organization.

For any transaction structure, there appear to be three possible transaction outcomes: transactions can be successfully completed, aborted, or side transactions can occur. But the likely paths from initiation of interaction between the boundary spanners to termination of interaction and the possibilities of alternative outcomes depends upon the type of transaction structure. Four types of transaction structures are possible, varying according to whether or not the boundary spanner is programmed, or can act heuristically and whether or not the nonmember is compelled or not compelled to interact with the boundary spanner. From the point of view of a particular organization, the easiest, and least threatening, transaction structure is one in which the boundary spanner is programmed and the nonmember is compelled to participate. This kind of "bureaucratic" transaction structure is appropriate for many kinds of clerical activities, such as the issuance of automobile plates and drivers' licenses. Examples of transaction structures where the boundary spanner's behavior is not programmed and the nonmember is not compelled to participate include private hospitals and voluntary social service agencies—with many of the services provided by private practitioners. Thompson suggests that, with each transaction structure, the stage is set for a three-person game, with the organization's managment always hoping that alliances that form will include the supervisor of the boundary spanner and the spanner and not develop between the spanner and the nonmember (Thompson, 1962, pp. 309–322).

Boundary spanning may be *ad hoc* and informal, e.g., developing when the need occurs, or it can be more formal and permanent. Examples of these two kinds of spanning are portrayed in Figures 5-1 and 5-2. As shown in Figure 5-1, each organization includes the dominant coalition (which has the power to decide the organization's strategies), constituents who have less power than the dominant coalition, and boundary spanners (Child, 1972). Members of the dominant coalition may be included among the boundary spanners. In Figure 5-1 the boundary spanning involves persons from the three organizations who interact with their counterparts from other organizations. These boundary spanners might be meeting informally to exchange information about the needs of their organizations, to discuss some expert personnel that one organization will loan to others for a short time, or to discuss a joint budget request they wish to present to a potential funder, such as the city council or the board of supervisors. Informal and *ad hoc* relations between boundary spanners are quite common in networks. The situation shown in Figure 5-2 is different because the boundary spanners serve on a coordinating committee. Coordinating committees are frequently used in the public and private sectors. Committees are examples of interstitial groups because they link diverse organizations in the community through coordination and exchange relations. If committees have resources to distribute, if proposals made by particular organizations must be reviewed and evaluated by the committees, or if the coordinating committees are trying to promote joint projects to be sponsored by several organizations, the organizations may experience some loss of autonomy. The control of boundary spanners by their organizations may be more problematic in the situations depicted in Figure 5-2 because their behavior may be less visible and because, over time, the boundary spanners will have more chance to influence one another.

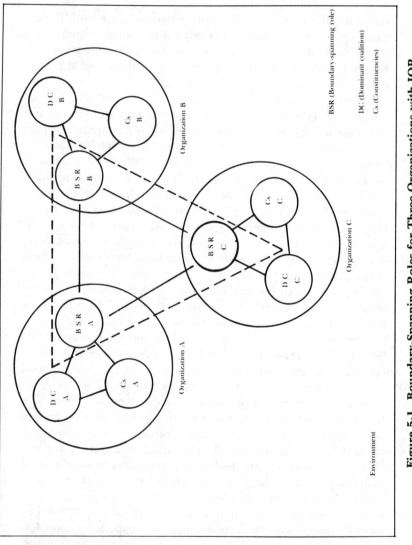

Figure 5-1. Boundary-Spanning Roles for Three Organizations with IOR.

BSR (Boundary-spanning role)

DC (Dominant coalition)

Cs (Constituencies)

116

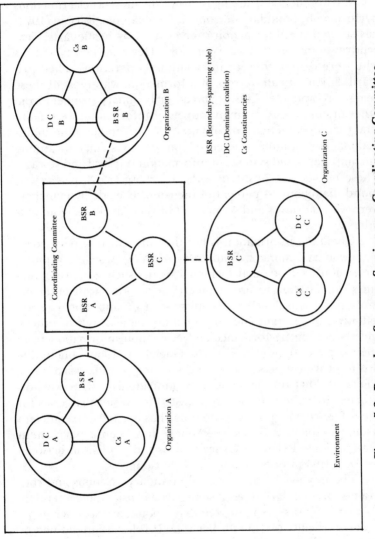

BSR (Boundary-spanning role)

DC (Dominant coalition)

Cs Constituencies

Figure 5-2. Boundary Spanners Serving on a Coordinating Committee.

117

Environmental scanning is one of the most crucial functions performed by boundary personnel. For example, Keegan (1974) has studied the information sources used by headquarters executives in multinational corporations. Headquarters executives who were responsible for international operations relied primarily upon human sources of information, with most of these being corporation executives abroad or boundary spanners from other organizations. Human sources of information were more vital than documentary or physical sources. Indeed, the multinational corporations studied seldom used systematic scanning or computer-based systems of information retrieval and storage. These results are consistent with Mintzberg (1973, p. 45) who found that about 44 percent of the contacts made by managers were with outsiders and 43 percent of their mail was from outsiders.

Obtaining information is not the only function performed by boundary spanners. Boundary spanning, which is a multidimensional activity, may include activities such as representing one's organization to nonmembers, negotiating with other organizations, traveling to meetings as an organizational representative, integrating and coordinating the activities of others, and requesting performance and evaluation information from other organizations (Miles, 1976). Guetzkow (1966), among the first to provide a perspective for discussing boundary spanning, points out that the designation of individuals with powers-of-attorney to act for business has existed in Western societies for ages. The role of political diplomat has existed since ancient Greece or before. Since 1949 there has been a permanent Congressional Relations Office that provides a liaison between the Department of State and the U.S. Congress.

The unique characteristics of boundary positions and constraints on boundary roles have received considerable attention. Role strain exists to the degree that a boundary spanner experiences difficulty playing his/her role. If roles are undefined by supervisors or expectations are vague, role ambiguity may result. Role conflict exists to the degree that simultaneous and conflicting expectations exist for boundary spanners. Role conflict may result if the expectations of other boundary spanners clash with the expectations of supervisors or constituents. It has been suggested (Katz and Kahn, 1978, pp. 204–206) that the side effects of role ambiguity and role conflict may be similar, including low job satisfaction, tension, low self-confidence, and poor job performance.

EFFORTS TO CONTROL SPANNERS AND ELIMINATE DEVIANCE

Efforts by organizations to help reduce the likelihood of role conflict and role ambiguity serve two distinct functions. To the degree that these aspects of role strain are eliminated, personal benefits will result for the boundary spanner. Behavior on the part of the boundary spanners that runs counter to organizational expectations and norms (deviant behavior) may also occur less frequently when roles are clear and expectations do not conflict. Because of the nature of boundary roles, however, it may be impossible to remove all sources of role strain, a situation that may not even be desirable. Some role innovation by boundary spanners may be very functional, especially when unexpected or unusual situations are encountered. Because relationships between boundary spanners from different organizations are not as much subject to authority as relationships within organizations, boundary spanners may have to accommodate one another and show some appreciation for differing points of view in order to work successfully.

Organizations do use protective devices to control boundary spanners and to help boundary spanners avoid role strain. For example, it has been suggested that boundary spanners should be thoroughly indoctrinated in terms of current organizational goals, priorities, and procedures. Uniforms, it is suggested, may help boundary spanners maintain their identification with the organization. Deliberate periodic shifting of personnel from one location to another, or from one set of clients to others, may be helpful in preventing unwanted identification with other organizations in the environment (Guetzkow, 1966, pp. 21–22). Other protective devices include periodic "inspirational" meetings held for sales forces in business and regulations that specifically regulate the length of foreign duty tours (Adams, 1976). In order to identify persons who possess requisite interpersonal skills and desired attributes to be good boundary spanners, it has been proposed that organizations may wish to develop programs to identify and better train future boundary spanners (Organ, 1971). Interestingly enough, this almost never occurs. For example, many of the persons reading this chapter have had some formal training in business, law, social work, or education. But I ask you this, how much of the training content was oriented towards helping you be a more effective boundary spanner? Most of the training was probably intended to help you learn how to be effective and get ahead within particular organizations.

Organizations sometimes maintain such permanent and lasting connections with each other that it is possible to make the roles for boundary spanners routine e.g., to regularize and control their behavior through roles and regulations that reduce the likelihood of deviance and role conflict or ambiguity. For example, Guetzkow (1966, pp. 18–20) describes desk clerks in national embassies whose roles in their day-to-day activities are defined by elaborate codes. These desk clerks should suffer relatively little role tension.

To some limited degree, many people in organizations engage in some boundary spanning. In particular, organizations with a mediating technology (Thompson, 1967, pp. 15–18) have the highest proportion of boundary roles. Organizations with a mediating technology link clients or customers with each other, and boundary spanners serve a "line" and not a staff function. For example, boundary spanners serve a line function in people-processing organizations such as schools, social service agencies, and government agencies (Aldrich and Herker, 1977, pp. 222–223).

When is boundary spanning officially recognized as part of one's job, and when do organizations make efforts to routinize boundary spanning? It has been suggested that the more critical the contingency, the more likely will boundary roles be explicitly formalized and care given to the selection of persons to play boundary roles. Aldrich and Herker (pp. 224–225) found in their review of the literature that roles such as labor negotiators and corporate lawyers responsible for labor relations are formally designated. In addition, recruiters of new corporation members, persons who serve as a buffer between full-time staff and the public (such as board members), corporation executives who manage reciprocal relations with large firms, and executives who pursue leads on possible acquisitions of other companies have formalized boundary-spanning roles.

Sometimes boundary spanners are given discretion in terms of how they play their roles, but at other times roles are routinized. What factors are associated with role discretion? Thompson (1962, pp. 311–312; 1967, p. 71) has identified two organizational characteristics and one environmental condition that partly determine the degree to which boundary roles are specified and made routine. Organizations that provide services to large numbers of persons—and therefore face many nonmembers relative to each boundary role—and those that employ a mechanized production technology that places a premium on large sums of standardized transactions per member at the output boundary are more likely to routinize roles. In addition, organizations that face stable environments are more likely to routinize boundary roles and grant role incumbents less discretion.

A typology of boundary-spanning activity has been developed based upon organizational need for information and perceived level of uncertainty of the environment such that combinations of the two factors determine the kind of boundary-spanning activity. Based upon this typology, propositions about boundary-spanning activity have been specified. It is thought that when organizational need for information is anticipated and regular, control over which members play boundary roles will be regulated. When need for information is unanticipated and occurs at irregular times, control over "who" plays boundary roles will not be regulated. Discretion permitted incumbents of boundary roles is thought to depend upon the degree to which the environment is perceived as uncertain. With low environmental uncertainty, persons are encouraged to follow specified routines that specify "how" they will interact with persons who are nonmembers. When environments are perceived as more uncertain, persons are not required to follow routines in their interaction with nonmembers. In summary, initiation of bound-ary-spanning activity (the "who" issue) is thought to depend pri-marily upon whether informal needs are anticipated and regular or unanticipated and irregular. On the other hand, the rou-tineness of boundary-spanning activity (the "how" issue) is thought to depend upon whether the environment is perceived as certain or uncertain (Leifer and Delbecq, 1978, pp. 44–47).

Factors Thought to Influence Interaction Between Boundary Spanners

We are concerned here with the outcomes from interaction between boundary spanners from different organizations. We are interested in outcomes for the boundary spanners and for their respective organizations. A re-examination of Figures 5-1 and 5-2 provides us with categories of variables that may influ-ence interaction outcomes. Relevant variables include the attri-butes of the respective organizations, constituents within orga-nizations, dominant coalitions, the attributes of the boundary spanners, and the environments within which the organizations are located. In addition, is the interaction *ad hoc* and perhaps limited in scope, as depicted in Figure 5-1? Or is the interaction more permanent and lasting?

Adams (1976) has made a major contribution to our un-derstanding of boundary-spanning roles and interaction between spanners in his integration of the literature. Adams singled out a number of variables thought to be especially crucial, reviewed empirical research, and offered a number of propositions about boundary spanning. Our goal is to summarize some of the most important observations made by Adams. Try to think again about the network of organizations that serve delinquent and prede-linquent youth (discussed in Chapter 4) or keep in mind bound-ary spanners in another network with which you are familiar. Ask yourself, how do these variables affect boundary spanners? Are there other variables that are important, too?

In their pioneering study of boundary roles, Kahn, Wolfe, Quinn, Rosenthal, and Snoek (1964, pp. 115–116) found that boundary role persons do report a higher level of role tension than persons who play other roles. However, they found that persons who were frequent boundary spanners reported less role tension. Kahn et al. explained the relatively low role tension for frequent boundary spanners in terms of personnel selection that places people in boundary roles, trial and error factors, or the adaptation of organizational machinery. Organ (1971) has observed, however, that the findings of Kahn and colleagues may be due to the fact that persons who are frequent spanners are more likely to be removed from the surveillance and control of constituents. In his study of boundary spanners conducted in a laboratory setting, Organ tested and found support for his proposition that deviance by spanners was inversely related to the degree that the spanners thought their behavior was visible to their constituents.

Adams, who taught Organ and others who have written about boundary roles, has maintained contact with these students, and this continued dialogue has stimulated considerable theory and research. Adams, after considering Organ's findings and related research, concludes that the relative visibility of a boundary spanner's behavior may directly influence the spanner's flexibility when relating to persons from other organizations. It should be added that visibility depends somewhat upon the nature of the interaction setting. We would probably find that *ad hoc* interaction with persons from other organizations is generally less visible to constituents and the dominant coalition than interaction in coordinating committees (Figures 5-1 and 5-2). Committee meetings that are open to the public, minutes that are kept and made available, and the distribution of reports that describe committee activities and decisions will also increase the visibility of participants' behavior.

Organizations typically have implicit or explicit norms that reflect the ways that boundary spanners are encouraged to interact with members of other organizations. For example, the norms may emphasize cooperative or competitive behavior. The norms may encourage spanners to take a short or a long time perspective, e.g., only a few interactions may be expected or the norms may be such that interaction over an extended period of time is expected. Finally, the norms may indicate that the boundary spanner should take a flexible or an inflexible approach.

In addition to the organizational norms that influence boundary spanners, their perceptions of other boundary spanners' propensity to be exploitative or reasonable in bargaining has been shown to have an effect on behavior. For example, Frey and Adams (1972) have found in their simulated labor-management negotiation research that persons who were forced to interact with others who acted exploitatively sent those persons much more demanding messages than did persons who interacted with a cooperative person.

There may not be a consensus among constituents with regard to bargaining norms. Divisiveness among one's constituents, or perceived divisiveness among another boundary spanner's constituents, is thought to have an effect on a boundary spanner's behavior. When one's constituents do not agree, a person may feel released from having to conform to organizational norms. When it is known that the constituents of a boundary spanner from another organization are not in agreement, this may mean to the person that his interaction partner has some choices that the person can make in his behavior. Time pressure placed on boundary spanners to complete transactions obviously will have an effect on their behavior, too. In general, it is expected that time pressures on boundary spanners will lead to increased concessions. If time pressures are not the same for everyone, the boundary spanner faced with the strongest time pressure may be the most constrained.

In addition to these factors, the attractiveness of membership, or desire to retain membership, is also thought to influence the behavior of boundary spanners. Boundary spanners who are strongly attached to their organizations may be more influenced by organizational norms. Low attractiveness, on the other hand, may lead to more concessions when one's interaction partner is tough and competitive. These ideas suggest that boundary spanners who have considerable tenure in their organizations, or who have relatively few career options, may be reluctant to deviate from the expectations of constituents.

In the research mentioned earlier in this section, Organ (1971) had expected to find that boundary spanners who perceived greater trust had been placed in them by their constituents would be more likely to deviate from their constituents' expectations when necessary. However, Organ actually found no significant relationship between perceived trust and deviance. But research does provide some support for the trust hypothesis (Adams, 1976, pp. 1181–1193). Other variables that may influence interaction between boundary spanners include the relative power of their organizations, the degree that mutual dependence exists compared to asymmetric dependence, and changes that occur in the environment. Hopefully, this discussion has shed some light upon the importance of boundary roles, boundary spanning, and the kinds of role tension that boundary spannners may experience. Some of the hypotheses about boundary spanning, however, have never been subject to empirical evaluation, and many of the studies cited herein were laboratory studies, studies conducted in simulated organizational settings, or studies of bargaining and negotiation that do not bear directly on IOR. Fortunately, more studies of boundary spanning in real organizational settings are being conducted. What do these empirical studies show us about boundary roles and boundary spanning?

EMPIRICAL RESULTS

The importance of boundary roles is clearly underscored by the expanding literature. One specific way of determining the impact of boundary roles for specific organizations is to have other organizational members evaluate the roles played by incumbents of boundary positions. Wall and Adams (1974), who studied the evaluations of salesmen by members of their own organization, have found that favorable evaluations are based upon obedience to evaluator's directives rather than to the market's receptiveness to products. In other words, in some situations, conformity to the expectations of other members is the shortest path to social status and esteem for boundary spanners.

Another way of looking at boundary spanners, relative to

other members, is to ask about the amount of power associated with boundary positions. Interestingly enough, the environment has much to do with the power of boundary spanners. First, it has been shown that forces in the environment determine the amount of power that organizations concentrate in boundary units. In a study of collective bargaining involving 228 locals of the International Association of Firefighters and city governments around the country, Kochan (1975) found that the amount of power that organizations concentrate in boundary-spanning units depends primarily upon the amount of power other organizations have invested in their respective boundary units. This finding supports the countervailing power hypothesis developed by Thompson (1967).

In addition to the need for countervailing power, it has been suggested that the greater the perceived environmental uncertainty of constituents, the more power they will attribute to those who play boundary roles. This hypothesis is based upon the idea that as environments become turbulent and unstable, the information-processing function of boundary positions becomes central to an organization's ability to be effective. Empirical research confirms this hypothesis. In his study of purchasing agents in 20 firms representing 11 different industries, Spekman (1979, pp. 111–113) found that his findings supported the positive relationship between the level of perceived uncertainty and the power attributed to purchasing agents. Resource dependency was a relevant notion in this context, too. It was found that constituents operating under conditions of greater uncertainty perceive purchasing agents to exercise influence even in issues not directly related to purchasing. This results because purchasing agents in their gatekeeper role sit at the juncture of many communication paths.

Questions about the amount of role tension for boundary positions and the determinants of role tension have by far dominated the empirical research conducted during the 1970s. Is it true that incumbents of boundary positions are particularly prone to role tension? What causes role tension?

The research conducted by Keller and his associates has focused upon information functions performed by boundary spanners. Keller and Holland (1975) have conducted a study of 51 professionals located in a large government research and development organization. Boundary-spanning scores were based upon four related activites:

1. number of journals, magazines, and newspapers regularly read,

2. frequency with which the subject recommended specific information sources to colleaques,

3. frequency with which the subjects sought information/advice from members of other organizations, and

4. the frequency with which persons from other organizations sought the subjects' information/advice.

Contrary to expectations, boundary spanning was actually related negatively to role ambiguity and positively to job satisfaction. Role conflict was not significantly related to the amount of boundary spanning. The effects of boundary spanning appear to depend upon the relative rank of persons considered.

In their study of 192 managerial, engineering, and supervisory personnel located in one large company, Keller, Szilagyi, Jr. & Holland (1976) found that boundary spanning was associated with role ambiguity only for supervisors. While boundary spanning was positively related to measures of job satisfaction for managers and engineers, it was negatively related to job satisfaction for supervisors. In other words, boundary spanning appears to be an important and desirable component of higher occupational positions. As originally predicted by Kahn et al. (1964), boundary spanning takes on negative aspects only at the lower level of supervision. Persons at higher occupational levels do more boundary spanning, and boundary spanning itself leads to an increase in job variety, autonomy, task identity, and friendship opportunities for these persons. These authors also suggest that the information possessed by boundary spanners, which is not available to others, may be the source of their power in organizations.

Because the degree to which boundary positions are visible to constituents is thought to be crucial, Cox, Hitt, and Stanton (1978) sought to determine if the number of organizational boundaries, intraorganizational and interorganizational, that separate boundary spanners from persons in their role set was related to role tension. This measure of "organizational distance" was not significantly related to role ambiguity for persons at any level in the organization. "Organizational distance" was negatively related to role conflict for persons at the top level in the organization.

The measure of boundary spanning used by Keller and his associates has been severely criticized by Miles (1976) who has pointed out that only the information-processing function was stressed by them. In Miles' study of 142 persons occupying five distinct professional level roles in nine government research and development organizations, he used a measure of boundary spanning that included information processing, representation, transactional, and integrative aspects of boundary spanning. Miles found that persons who did more boundary spanning did have higher role conflict but not higher role ambiguity, regardless of their rank in the organization. Like Keller and his associates, Miles found that the benefits of boundary spanning may offset the costs. Persons who did more boundary spanning had higher job satisfaction, greater self-assurance, and reported better interpersonal relations with co-workers.

Despite the fact that top-level administrators devote a considerable portion of their time to relations with other organizations, interorganizational factors have not been included in models of role tension. In their study of administrators in 110 county offices of federal, state, and county agencies, Rogers and Molnar (1976, pp. 604–608) sought to determine if interorganizational contacts or organizational variables contributed most to role tension. Interorganizational variables tended to be more important in determining role conflict than organizational factors. For example, the more subjects reported that they were "pressured" from sources outside their own organization, and the more that they served on boards of other organizations, the more their role conflict. Serving on boards was also one of the few interorganizational variables that was positively related to role ambiguity. The more that directors of agencies interacted with directors from other organizations, the less their role conflict or ambiguity. On the whole, organizational variables were more important than intraorganizational variables in causing role ambiguity. Administrators with less formal education and training were much more likely to suffer role ambiguity, and freedom is associated with costs. That is, administrators who reported that they had autonomy in spending unbudgeted money and altering work responsibilities of specialists and staff reported both higher role conflict and role ambiguity.

In summary, Rogers and Molnar found that intraorganizational variables, as a whole, were related to role ambiguity but not to role conflict, although some of the individual organizational variables were related to role conflict. Interorganizational variables, as a whole, however, were related to both role conflict and role ambiguity. It was concluded that although these administrators have ability to adjust to inconsistent or competing demands from within their own organizations, they may not be equally well qualified to function with boundary spanners from other organizations in the absence of bureaucratic structure. In particular, higher levels of role tension tended to be associated with IOR involving moderate or higher levels of resource commitment and with participation of members of other organizations in the decision making of an agency.

SUMMARY

The human element cannot be removed from an analysis of IOR that occur in the community. Boundary spanners play crucial roles for their respective organizations and boundary spanning is an important aspect of the job, especially for higher level positions where people do relatively more boundary spanning. In spite of the fact that boundary spanning has been thought to cause role tension, including role ambiguity and role conflict, empirical research shows that this is not the case for higher level positions. Boundary spanning is associated with role tension only for persons in lower level positions. Organizations concentrate power in boundary units to the degree needed to match the power of boundary units in other organizations. Boundary spanners are attributed power by their constituents because of the information they possess that is helpful in reducing uncertainty. Constituents prefer boundary spanners who do not deviate from organizational expectations, and is an absence of other data, equate effectiveness with conformity. Much remains to be known about boundary roles and boundary spanning. The needed research that is sure to follow in the 1980s will be most welcome to specialists and to persons in the community with applied interests.

DISCUSSION QUESTIONS

1. How do boundary-spanning roles differ from other organization roles?

2. Why are boundary spanners thought to be especially prone to role strain?

3. To what degree do empirical studies support the proposition that boundary spanner will suffer role strain?

4. Give some examples of transaction structures in your community.

5. What functions do boundary spanners provide for organizations?

6. Talk to a boundary spanner. What formal or informal training, if any, did this person receive to help prepare him/her for his/her role?

7. Why and how do organizations attempt to control boundary spanners?

8. What determines who plays boundary-spanning roles and how they are played?

9. What can managers do to aid and support those who play boundary-spanning roles?

10. What is the most important unanswered question about boundary spanners that should next be considered by researchers?

A FICTITIOUS CASE STUDY: NO PROMOTION FOR BILL SMITH

The J.W. Watson store is located in Wheeling, a city of 700,000 population. J.W. Watson is one of three large stores that dominate the metropolitan area. Two branch stores of J.W. Watson have been developed in suburban shopping malls. The two suburban store managers and the manager of the original store, still located in the central business district, meet with each other and the president of the board of J.W. Watson on a regular basis to discuss market trends, seasonal buying, advertising, personnel matters, and so on.

Dick Jones is the current president of the board. Tom Taylor manages the central store, Tim Logan manages the store in Willowrun Mall, and Charles Lee manages the store in the Appletown Mall. Tom Taylor enjoys the current situation very much. All three stores are doing well, his store is still tops in total sales, and he finds his relationships with the other two store managers and with top management very satisfying. Buying trips have always been exciting for him. Tom finds it interesting to bargain with retail supply agents for the best prices that he can obtain and to obtain quality merchandise. Tom Taylor is well known by other retail managers in the region, and he has made presentations at regional conventions.

Bill Smith is one of our department managers supervised by Tom Taylor. Bill Smith has been with the store for 10 years and was promoted to the position of acting departmental manager for men's clothing one year ago. During his annual review last week, however, Bill Smith was told by Tom Taylor that his position was not secure and that he would not be made department manager at this time. Smith was told that he lacked aggressiveness, was hesitant when making decisions about his department, and had not made a good impression on personnel from other J.W. Watson stores. In addition, Smith was criticized, although Taylor said this was not a serious concern, for not being involved enough in community service organizations. The J.W. Watson stores have been in the community for many years and management has been proud of its reputation for community participation.

Bill Smith is quite unhappy and frustrated because of his bad news. Taylor has told Smith that he wants to get together with Smith to map out some remedial and corrective action because he wants Smith to be successful. But Smith wonders if the plan will really help him. Because of an error he made when placing an order with a supplier of men's suits earlier in the year, Smith has been told by Taylor to be certain to have Taylor's approval before placing orders in the future. Smith had been told earlier, too, that he was premature in giving a salary increase to a clerk who worked under his supervision. Smith likes to interact with personnel from other stores, and to share ideas, but he has been cautioned by Taylor not to make decisions or promises that will commit the store until Smith can "check signals back home." Smith does belong to a community service organizaton but attends only rarely. Smith is reluctant to take on too much service work because his days are already long and demanding. Smith has been reprimanded by Taylor for spending too much time on the telephone talking about a community service project and for being late in getting back to the store from a luncheon meeting at the service club.

QUESTIONS FOR CASE ANALYSIS

1. Smith wonders if he should try to get some advice from the department managers, of if he should just try harder. What do you think?

2. Smith has thought about quitting. Are Smith's problems caused mostly by his own personal characteristics or by other factors?

3. What solutions would you propose?

REFERENCES

Adams, J. S. The structure and dynamics of behavior in organizational boundary roles. In M. D. Dunnette (Ed.), *Handbook of industrial and organizational psychology.* Chicago: Rand McNally, 1976, pp. 1175–1199.

Aldrich, H. E., & Herker, D. Boundary spanning roles and organization structure. *The Academy of Management Review,* 1977, *2,* 217–230.

Child, J. Organizational structure, environment and performance: The role of strategic choice. *Sociology,* 1972, *6,* 1–22.

Cox, J. A., Hitt, M. A., & Stanton, W. W. An Examiniation of the Relationship of Boundary Spanning Relevance to Hierarchical Level, Perceived Environmental Uncertainty and Role Stress. Academy of Management Proceedings, San Francisco, CA. August, 1978, pp. 175–179.

Frey, R. L., Jr., & Adams, J. S. The negotiator's dilemma: Simultaneous in-group and outgroup conflict. *Journal of Experimental Social Psychology,* 1972, *4,* 331–346.

Guetzkow, H. Relations among organizations. In R. V. Bowers (Ed.), *Studies on behavior in organizations.* Athens, GA: University of Georgia Press, 1966, pp. 13–44.

Kahn, R. L., Wolfe, D. M., Quinn, R. P., Rosenthal, R. A., & Snoek, J. D. *Organizational stress.* New York: John Wiley and Sons, 1964.

Katz, D., & Kahn, R. L. *The social psychology of organizations.* New York: John Wiley and Sons, 1978.

Keegan, W. Multinational scanning: A study of information sources utilized by headquarters executives in multinational companies. *Administrative Science Quarterly,* 1974, *19,* 411–421.

Keller, R. T., & Holland W. E. Boundary spanning roles in a research and development organization: An empirical investigation. *Academy of Management Journal,* 1975, *18,* 388–393.

Keller, R. T., Szilagyi, A. D., Jr., & Holland, W. E. Boundary-spanning activity and employee reactions: An empirical study. *Human Relations,* 1976, *29,* 699–710.

Kochan, T. A. Determinants of the power of boundary units in an interorganizational bargaining relation. *Administrative Science Quarterly,* 1975, *20*, 434–452.

Leifer, R., & Delbecq, A. Organizational/environmental interchange: A model of boundary spanning activity. *The Academy of Management Review,* 1978, *3*, 40–50.

Miles, R. H. Individual differences in a model of organizational role stress: An empirical investigation. *Journal of Business Research,* 1976, *4*, 87–102.

Mintzberg, H. *The nature of managerial work.* New York: Harper and Row, 1973.

Organ, D. Linking pins between organizations and environments. *Business Horizons,* 1971, *14*, 73–80.

Rogers, D. L., & Molnar, J. J. Organizational antecedents of role conflict and ambiguity in top-level administrators. *Administrative Science Quarterly,* 1976, *21*, 598–610.

Spekman, R. Influence and information: An exploratory investigation of the boundary role person's basis of power. *Academy of Management Journal,* 1979, *22*, 104–117.

Thompson, J. D. Organizations and output transactions. *American Journal of Sociology,* 1962, *68*, No. 2, 309–324.

———*Organizations in action.* New York: McGraw-Hill, 1967.

Wall, J. A., Jr., & Adams, J. S. Some variables affecting constituent's evaluation of and behavior toward a boundary role occupant. *Organizational Behavior and Human Performance,* 1974, *11*, 390–408.

Chapter 6

NETWORKS OF ORGANIZATIONS AND COLLECTIVE EFFORTS

We have seen that the goals and strategies of dominant co-alitions in particular organizations and the comparative (dyadic) properties of organizations provide considerable insights for our understanding of exchanges and conflict between organizations in the community. For example, we have learned in Chapter 4 that mutual dependence and frequent contact between organizations are associated with resource exchanges. Operating conflict is associated with resource scarcity, differences in formalization, and frequent contact between organizations. Greater understanding, however, requires our consideration of more comprehensive collectivities. Organizations do not exist in a social vacuum. We are interested in larger networks of organizations and in community-wide patterns of IOR for two reasons. First, networks, or community-wide patterns, may be analyzed in terms of their influence on particular organizations and on dyadic interaction. Secondly, consequences of network structure and processes can be determined in terms of policy outcomes and network effectiveness. In this chapter we will begin by becoming familiar with terminology and conceptual elements necessary for network analysis. Then, we will evaluate theoretical perspectives on networks. Methods for analyzing networks will be reviewed, followed by an examination of empirical research that has resulted from studies of networks and communities.

CONCEPTUAL ELEMENTS FOR NETWORK ANALYSIS

First, what do we mean by network? In his summary of network analysis, Mitchell (1969, p. 2) provides a working definition of a social network: "a specific set of linkages among a defined set of persons, with the additional property that the characteristics of these linkages as a whole may be used to interpret the social behavior of the persons involved." Because we are concerned with linkages that occur between people and organizations, following Laumann, Galaskiewicz, and Marsden (1978, p. 458), social networks are defined here as "a set of nodes (e.g., persons, organizations) linked by a set of social relationships (e.g., friendship, transfer of funds, overlapping membership) of a specific type."

It is necessary to keep in mind distinctions between organization sets, action sets, and networks. An action set consists of a number of organizations formed into a temporary alliance for a limited purpose. Reciprocity is a problem in action sets because leaders in some organizations may think that they are getting less out of an alliance than they are putting into it. The concept "organization set" (Evan, 1965) draws our attention to a specific focal organization and its relations with organizations that provide inputs or receive its outputs.

Aldrich has observed that the limited purpose of action sets means that the bonds linking the organizations are usually temporary. An interorganizational network, however, consists of all organizations linked, directly or indirectly, by a specific type of relation; the presence of networks is determined by finding the ties between all organizations in a population (Aldrich, 1979, pp. 280–281). Network analysis assumes that the ways in which nodes (persons or organizations) are connected to one another, both directly and indirectly, influence the behavior of particular nodes and the system as a whole (Laumann and Pappi, 1976, pp. 20–

21). Since the influence of organizational patterns ("fields") on the interaction between organizations and on the activity level and complexity of new relationships has been singled out as a high priority (Turk, 1969; Warren, 1967) a network perspective on the community seems very appropriate.

The three most basic elements of structure in network analysis are nodes, linkages between nodes, and modalities of network formation. Modalities of network formation describe the general normative context permeating a network, with the two major kinds of modality being competitive and cooperative (Laumann, et al., 1978, pp. 465–466). This notion of modes is very comparable to the conception of an institutionalized "thought structure" in communities that provides generally accepted rationales for relationships between organizations (Warren et al., 1975, pp. 179–180).

CONCEPTUALIZING THE COMMUNITY AS A NETWORK OF IOR

An adequate theoretical discussion of interorganizational networks in the community must address three issues or questions:

1. By what processes are interorganizational linkages formed and maintained?

2. Through what mechanisms are partial or total networks mobilized for collective action?

3. How do collective decisions and action result from interorganizational activation (Laumann et al., 1978)?

Networks today are most often conceived of in terms of resource dependence theory or in terms of a political economy, in which case greater emphasis is placed upon the impact of external forces in the network's environment, e.g., influences from funding sources, regulatory agencies, and legal mandates. In reviewing these two conceptions of networks we will see that the three requirements raised by Laumann and colleagues have not received equal attention.

Formation and Maintenance of Linkages in Networks

The political economic model of networks (Benson, 1975; Galaskiewicz, 1979; Zald, 1970) and the resource dependence model of networks (Aldrich, 1979; Pfeffer and Salancik, 1978; Van de Ven, 1980) do focus explicitly on how networks are formed and maintained. Because organizations frequently lack needed resources or must find available markets for their products or services, relationships must be established with other organizations. In addition, organizations that compete for resources or provide comparable services or products are also interdependent. Yuchtman and Seashore (1967) were among the first to observe that organization decision makers are oriented toward the acquisition of scarce resources.

It has been suggested that networks of exchange that are loosely coupled may be most adaptable. With loosely coupled networks, organizations within subsystems may be richly joined, e.g., have multiple relationships with other organizations within the subnetwork units but with fairly weak or minimal relationships between subnetwork units. Richly coupled systems without subsystems would have difficulty reaching stable states, and change affecting any relationship might affect all relationships. Aldrich suggests that networks in complex, heterogenous, and changing environments will most likely be loosely coupled. Other organizatons or action sets in networks are the major sources of constraints for organizations because they frequently control more resources than individuals or unorganized elements. Dependencies develop between organizations in networks because of unequal access to resources (Aldrich, 1979, pp. 325–327). The political economic model, we have observed, differs from the resouce dependence model in the importance that it attributes to extranetwork linkages.

Not only may some organizations or subnetwork units gain power relative to others because of favorable internal structure linkages, but some may also gain power because of their linkages to important units external to the network. Within the network, organizations that provide services vital to a large number of organizations may gain power because of their centrality. Organizations that are at the center of referral flow will gain power. For example, it has been observed that state employment agencies may gain power in some networks because they may receive clients from a number of action or social service agencies. Interorganizational dominance may also result because some organizatons have ties with powerful units outside the network that provide resources and/or direction for network activities. If this is true, power relations in networks cannot be fully understood without attention to forces outside the network.

Benson maintains that money and authority are two of the most basic resources sought by organizations (Benson, 1975, pp. 229–233). Galaskiewicz (1979, pp. 1346–1347) who has studied community-wide networks thinks that money, information, and moral support are especially important resources. But Benson and Galaskiewicz agree that structural patterns in networks develop because of a competitive process in which organizations meet their needs through the exchange of resources.

Mobilization of Networks for Collective Action

Laumann et al. (1978) are correct in their contention that the mobilization of subnetwork units or whole networks must occur if such units are to influence the outcomes of community issues and collective actions. Such processes of mobilizaton may involve coalition formation or the mobilization of the network as a whole. Unfortunately, Laumann and his colleagues are also correct when they say that to this point in time, interorganizational theory has not seriously considered this issue, and it is difficult to locate empirical studies giving systematic attention to the topic (1978, pp. 472–473).

What motivates the dominant coalition (Child, 1972, pp. 14) in organizations to participate in collective action? Laumann et al. (1978, pp. 472–474) indicate that the following motives exist: self-interest, participation based upon the promise of future events, and the threat of negative sanctions. Aldrich (1979, p. 317) also stresses three motives: attractive incentives for participation, threats of coercion, and the presence of values stressing collective cooperation.

The private sector is a rich laboratory in which one can observe a wide variety of kinds of collective responses. Economists have labeled implicitly coordinated actions in the private sector as "interfirm organizations." Phillips (1960, pp. 605–610) and Williamson (1965, pp. 580–582) have tried to identify factors related specifically to interfirm behavior. Phillips has identified some conditions under which oligopolies (environments in which a small number of organizations possess enough power to influence collective decisions and actions) must use formal and centralized organizational structures in order to effectively concentrate their power and promote coordination. First, the larger the number of organizations involved, the more the need for formal planning and coordination. In addition, the better organized the groups from which purchases are made and to which sales are made, the more the need for centralized and formal interfirm organization. Two factors encourage a low degree of formality and coordination: an asymmetrical distribution of power among the organizations involved in interfirm behavior and adherence to a common set of values. Williamson has suggested that the munificence of the environment is a major factor causing organizations to shift from cooperative behavior to conflict. Williamson has also highlighted the importance of communication, which is a prerequisite for interfirm behavior.

Pfeffer and Salancik (1978, pp. 143–182) have provided a very vivid analysis of a wide variety of collective actions including interlocking directorates, joint ventures, normative constraints on activity, and coordination through centralized structures such as trade associations and cartels. They conclude that the single best predictor of the need for and feasibility of interfirm activity is interfirm communication. Although the focus of Pfeffer and Salancik is primarily upon business organizations in their analysis, they provide many illustrations of behavior akin to interfirm behavior in the public sector too. For example, the United Fund can be seen as a kind of cartel, attempting to organize and co-

ordinate social service agencies in the community to avoid competition for donations and to reduce excessive overlapping of
services. Trade associations are formed to provide the essential
centralized information and coordination required in uncon-
centrated industries. American psychologists formed the Association for the Advancement of Psychology in 1974 in response
to threats and external pressures. The American Medical Association and the American Psychiatric Association has been attempting to have the treatment of mental illness defined as a
clinical practice limited to medical personnel, which would greatly
harm the business of many clinical psychologists (Pfeffer and
Salancik, 1978, pp. 177–180). If collusion between organizations
is functional for the organizations involved and if a set of interdependent organizations might adversely affect each other's
performance without resorting to negotiated environments, why
is collective action so frequently seen as bad? Pfeffer and Salancik
conclude that the problem with negotiated environments is that
they probably do not include the interests of all parties, especially
the organizations with less power and capacity to organize (pp.
183–184).

Given the fact that few empirical studies of collective interorganizational mobilization have been completed and that theories are incomplete, where are we to turn in the short run for
guidelines? Two suggestions seem in order. First, increasingly,
studies of dyadic interaction between organizations are being
completed (see Chapter 4) and dyadic theories evaluated and
integrated. Although the dynamics of larger networks are undoubtedly more complex, persons who are interested in collective
responses should be fully aware of these studies of dyads. Secondly, although the research has not been conducted with organizations and has often been based upon contrived laboratory
settings, the vast literature on bargaining and negotiation offers
many suggestions and points to consider. In particular, the book
by Rubin and Brown (1975), in which they summarize and interpret the state of the art, is highly recommended. More than
500 articles published in approximately 40 different journals
from 1960 to 1974 are used in this review. For example, what
factors encourage the development of coalitions? What factors

tend to prevent the formation of coalitions? A large body of research suggests that coalitions are most likely to form when the
participants see advantages in joining with others to counter the
power of others. In addition, if another party is seen as a common
enemy, and if there is an initial proclivity toward cooperation,
unification against the common enemy is likely (pp. 69–70).
Three conditions inhibit the development of coalitions according
to Rubin and Brown: when the combined power of weaker parties is seen as insufficient to offset the power of others, when
sources of conflict among would-be partners exist, and when a
more powerful party can effectively block the development of
coalitions (1975, pp. 71–72). In addition, the evidence indicates
that relatively weak parties are more likely to seek each other
out as partners than they are to form alliance with parties having
much more power. The reasoning here is that the less powerful
party might be taken advantage of by powerful partners. In addition, parties that have already demonstrated their status, ability,
and skill are most likely to be included when alliances form. Finally, parties that have a reputation for success and the honoring
of prior coalition agreements are preferred (1975, pp. 72–78).

Transformation Processes

Warren (1967) has discussed alternative coordinated delivery
systems that range from unitary and centralized to federated
and coalitional. Nevertheless, the empirical literature on IOR
has examined the actual production of joint decisions and joint
implementation, for the most part only by inference (Laumann
et al., 1978, p. 477). We are primarily concerned here with interorganizational structure, e.g., how organizations relate to one
another when planning jointly or implementing a joint effort.
     Although case studies of coordination projects for the de-
livery of human services have been completed (Aiken, Dewar,
DiTomaso, Hage, and Zeitz, 1975; Gans and Horton, 1975), the
conceptualizing of collective decisions and implementation is
quite inadequate. Theory that conceives of networks or of whole
communities as input-throughput-output systems (Clark, 1973;
Laumann and Pappi, 1976; Turk, 1973) shows some promise.

Interorganizational relations are seen as elements of the "throughput" mechanism, which converts inputs into outputs. But much remains to be done. In some ways, theory for analyzing networks and collective efforts lags behind available methods for analyzing networks. As we will see in the next section, tools for analyzing network structure are especially available.

METHODS FOR NETWORK ANALYSIS

Tichy and Fombrun (1979) have provided us with a parsimonious list of the structural properties of networks of organizations and have developed very straightforward computational methods for measuring these properties. With some adaptation, these guidelines are very applicable for analyzing interorganizational networks. Some of the structural properties that may be most relevant for our purposes are adapted and presented in Table 6-1.

Graphs are commonly used to portray networks schematically, but matrices are most frequently used to describe complex networks. A graph is a set of points (or some other symbols such as circles) representing units joined by lines representing exchanges, positive evaluations, or conflict. Sociograms are graphs that have been developed to portray relationships between people, but these graphs can also be used for interorganizational analysis.

As presented in graphic or matrix form, a network is a static entity. The network pattern will vary, depending upon the specific linkage being analyzed: a pattern portraying information exchanges between organizations may be quite different from one portraying formal agreements or operational conflict. Because of these qualifications, great care must be taken when using graphs or matrices to interpret network structure. A sociogram for organizations in a hypothetical exchange network is presented in Figure 6-1. The graph, or sociogram, is represented in the matrix form of an adjacency matrix in Figure 6-2. Arrows are used in the sociogram to connect organizations having a relationship. For example, two-headed arrows connect organizations

Table 6-1. Selected Properties of Interorganizational Networks*

I. Overall Network Structure

    A. Size: Number of organizations in the network.

    B. Density: Proportion of organizations in the community that are members of the network.

    C. Connectedness: The extent to which organizations are linked to each other.

    D. Fit: Degree of overlap of networks based upon different kinds of linkages.

II. Clustering Within Networks

    A. Clustering: The number of cliques or subsets of organizations that are inter-connected.

    B. Overlap: The degree to which clusters overlap with each other.

    C. Openness: The proportion of links to organizations from outside a cluster.

    D. Connectedness: The extent to which organizations in a cluster are linked to each other.

III. Properties of Individual Organizations in Networks

    A. Key Organizations: Organizations with the greatest number of linkages.

    B. Liaisons: Organizations that connect two or more clusters but who are not members of any cluster.

    C. Bridges: Organizations that are members of more than one cluster.

---

*Adapted from Tichy and Fombrun, 1979, 928–929.

1 and 2, 1 and 3, and 2 and 3 in Figure 6-1. These two-headed arrows mean that the resource flows are symmetrical. On the other hand, the arrow from organization 2 to 6 and from 6 to 3 is used to show that resources were provided by 2 for 6 and by 6 to 3. Organizations 5 and 10 are isolates in this hypothetical network.

An adjacency matrix is developed by listing the organizations in the network along the rows and columns in the same order. The presence of a relationship is shown by a "1" in the cells and the absence by a "0," such that the row corresponds to the organizations initiating the choices, or interaction, or providing resources and the columns correspond to the organizations receiving the choices, or interaction, or resources.

Figure 6-2 illustrates the adjacency matrix that corresponds to Figure 6-1. The diagonals always contain 0's in the basic adjacency matrix because an organization doesn't choose or provide resources to itself. Looking across a row in Figure 6-2 indicates which organizations received resources. For example, a 1 is present in row 1, column 2 and row 1, column 3 to show that organizations 2, and 3 received resources from organization 1. The row totals provide a measure of the total number of organizatons that received resources from other organizations. We see from

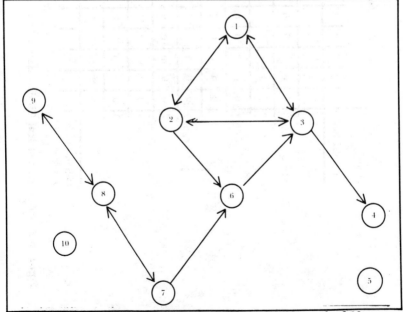

Figure 6-1. Sociogram of Exchange Among a Network of 10 Hypothetical Organizations.

To Organization

From Organization	1	2	3	4	5	6	7	8	9	10	Row Totals
1	0	1	1	0	0	0	0	0	0	0	2
2	1	0	1	0	0	1	0	0	0	0	3
3	1	1	0	1	0	0	0	0	0	0	3
4	0	0	0	0	0	0	0	0	0	0	0
5	0	0	0	0	0	0	0	0	0	0	0
6	0	0	1	0	0	0	0	0	0	0	1
7	0	0	0	0	0	1	1	0	0	0	2
8	0	0	0	0	0	0	1	1	0	0	2
9	0	0	0	0	0	0	0	0	1	0	1
10	0	0	0	0	0	0	0	0	0	0	0
Column Totals	2	2	3	1	0	2	2	2	1	0	14

Figure 6-2. An Asymmetrical Choice Matrix (R matrix) of a Network of 10 Hypothetical Organizations.

Figure 6-2 that two organizations received resources from organization 1. Reading down a column shows which organizations provided resources for each organization and the total number of organizations that provided resources. For example, we can see from the totals for columns 5 and 10 that these organizations were provided resources by no organizations.

A matrix (cooperation or conflict) may be binary, consisting of ones and zeros such as the ones presented in this chapter, or it may contain real numbers as entries. A binary matrix indicates only that some relation does or does not hold between two entities, while a real matrix may indicate the strength or type of relationship between them. A matrix may be asymmetrical, showing all choices that are initiated and received (the R matrix) or symmetrical, showing only mutual choices (the S matrix). Figure 6-2, which corresponds to Figure 6-1, is an example of an R matrix.

Many properties of networks, subnetworks, and individual organizations in networks can be derived directly from a graph or matrix. It is clear from Figures 6-1 and 6-2 that organizations 1, 2, and 3 form a subnetwork unit and so do organizations 2, 3, and 6. Units of people are sometimes called cliques and units of organizations are called blocks or clusters. However, if the network is fairly large and a number of subnetworks or "cliques" are present, the analysis is more difficult to do by inspection.

For comparison, consider the network of exchange relationships between voluntary organizations in "Rural·C," one of the communities studied by Mulford (1962). Figure 6-3 is a sociogram of actual relationships between voluntary organizations in a community of approximately 700. The network shown is much more complex than the hypothetical network presented in Figure 6-1. Subnetwork units exist with overlap between units, any many direct and indirect relationships exist. Clearly, more sophisticated analytical techniques than graphs are required for even moderately large networks.

A variety of computer programs are available for analyzing adjacency matrices. Tichy and Fombrun (1979, pp. 959–961) provide an excellent discussion of the merits of each computer program and provide examples of network analysis. These pro-

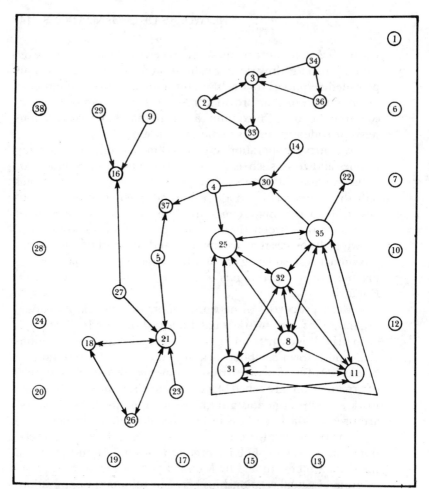

Figure 6-3. Sociogram of Exchange Relationships Among
Voluntary Organizations in "Rural C." [Adapted from
sociogram presented by Mulford (1962). Linkages to
organizations outside the community have been
eliminated.]

grams readily identify subnetworks (or cliques of organizations), number of direct and indirect linkages between organizations, and provide graphic portrayals of network structure. In addition, organizations that are the most "central" in networks are readily identified. Once subnetworks are identified, the researcher may wish to compare the characteristics of subnetworks relative to other subnetworks or the overall network.

In addition to measures of network properties developed directly from graphs or matrices, other measures of network properties have been developed in a few studies. Indeed, for large networks, the latter approach to measurement has many advantages. In the section that follows, when we consider the empirical studies of networks, the reader will have an opportunity to become familiar with these measurement efforts.

EMPIRICAL EXAMINATION OF NETWORKS: FOCUS UPON STRUCTURES AND OUTCOMES

We are interested here in reviewing empirical studies of the interorganizational structure of networks. Studies of dyads (see Chapter 4) are increasing in number and are helpful in understanding interorganizational structure. But our goal is to concentrate on those rare empirical studies that have emphasized the analysis of network structure. Existing studies of network structure can be divided into three categories: studies that have concentrated on structure, studies that have attempted to determine the impact of structure on dyadic relations, and studies that have attempted to link structural characteristics to network outputs. First, let's consider some of the tools used to describe network structures empirically.

The Structure of Networks

Participant observation combined with interviews conducted with network participants has been used in a number of network studies. Perruci and Pilisuk (1970) were among the first to conduct an empirical study demonstrating the linkage between organizations in a community and elite persons. Available organizational data and data obtained through interviews with persons identified as elite citizens were utilized in this analysis of a Midwestern community of 50,000. Elite persons holding executive positions in many organizations were different from other elites in five ways. "Interorganizational elites" were more likely to be named as involved in past community issues of major importance, be identified as having a general reputation for power, be similar in their views on community issues, see each other socially, and be identified as most powerful. Perrucci and Pilisuk were able to prove that access to top organizations can be seen as a key resource for elite persons; in other words that power can be viewed as a property of interorganizational ties. They were also able to demonstrate that a resource network existed in this community.

Warren, Bergunder, Newton, and Rose (1975) used a combination of both narrative and interview schedule data in their study of community decision organizations (CDOs) in nine cities. The interaction of these organizations was studied in the context of the Model Cities program in which each city participated. Mild cooperation was the most typical form of interaction found between CDOs in these cities. Few major changes were reported in either agency structure or programs because of Model Cities funding. Contest over domain was found to be minimal. The interorganizational field in these cities was described in terms of an "institutional thought structure" that served to minimize contest between organizations and to resist change. The thought structure is based upon a general consensus regarding the diagnosis of urban problems and on the kind of intervention such diagnosis calls for.

Aldrich (1972; 1976) has used data from interviews with agency directors and self-administered questionnaires completed by directors and professional staff of local state employment offices located in 24 communities in New York. The main objective of this study was to describe the nature of the interaction between the employment offices and the organizatons in their set. Although Aldrich used a pair-wise relationship between the local employment service and manpower organizations in its set, he drew important conclusions about the networks of organizations. In particular, Aldrich found that two variables were central to an understanding of these networks. First, the presence of an overarching federal authority and statutory guidelines meant that some relations were coerced and not voluntary. Secondly, the need for resources had more to do with explaining patterns of interaction than any other variable. Throughout Aldrich's analysis, indicators of domain consensus and positive sentiments fare very poorly as predictors of interaction. Aldrich's conclusion is that resource dependence is a valuable model for analyzing networks of relationships.

Aldrich's approach, in which he studied many networks, can be contrasted with Benson's (1975) intensive analysis of one interagency network of four manpower training organizations in a multicounty area. Benson conducted interviews with client contact workers, supervisory personnel in local offices of each agency, and state officials. This network was described as a political economy concerned with the distribution of two scarce resources: money and authority. The interorganizational network itself was seen linked to a larger environment consisting of authorities, legislative bodies, bureaus, and publics. The fundamental argument developed by Benson was that interactions between organizations at the service delivery level are determined primarily by resource acquisition processes. Organizations that are more central in the network structure and organizations that have linkages to elements in the larger environment are more powerful in the network. Relationships between domain consensus, ideological consensus, positive evaluations of organizations, and patterns of collaboration and cooperation between organizations are seen as important but are explained ultimately at the substructural (resource acquisition) level, according to Benson.

Adjacency matrices have also been used to analyze the structures of a few real networks. Raw data are obtained through interviews or questionnaires completed with organizational leaders or other respondents knowledgeable about the network. Laumann and Pappi (1976) have used adjacency matrices for elite persons and organizations to analyze the social structure of the German city "Altnevstadt." Utilizing a technique known as smallest space analysis, the adjacency matrices were manipulated in order to identify important subnetwork units and cleavages between these units. In addition, overlapping memberships of elite persons in subnetworks of organizations were determined. Graphic representation of Altnevstadt's community structure was developed and aided greatly in Laumann and Pappi's interpretation. The major weakness of this study, the authors point out (pp. 268), was the neglect of process and structural transformations over time, e.g., this picture of Altnevstadt was static and completed at only one point in time.

Galaskiewicz (1979) has used smallest space analysis to study the interorganizational structure of "Towertown," a community of 32,000 located in the Midwest. The target population of organizations included all industries, banks, savings and loans, newspapers, radio stations, service clubs, fraternal organizations, business associations, unions, law firms, health agencies, high schools, welfare agencies, churches, professional associations, county offices, municipal offices, and political parties. Utilizing a political economy framework (Benson, 1975; Zald, 1970), Galaskiewicz developed and analyzed propositions about the flow of three resources among the organizations, namely, money, information, and moral support. Data for the analysis of resource flows were obtained through interviews conducted with each organization's highest ranking person. Each informant was also asked to specify which organizations were most influential, with each organization's influence score being the total number of times it was mentioned as being very influential. Centrality scores for the organizations were computed from the adjacency matrices, and resource subnetworks were identifed.

Galaskiewicz reported that the amount of funds an organization controlled was the strongest predictor of centrality. Centrality in a resource network, in turn, was significantly related to perceived influence (Galaskiewicz, 1979, p. 1359). Local cash dependency was also important in determinig centrality. The money network was roughly divided into private and public sectors. The information network was clustered according to activities rather than auspices. The support network was organized in such a way that organizations representing collective values (such as health, education, and welfare) were clustered together. Galaskiewicz concludes with the important observation that the structural properties of the community are the by-products of the competition among organizations and will thus reflect the interests of the more resourceful actors in the community (pp. 1352–1361).

Block modeling is a technique in which data in adjacency matrices are manipulated in order to develop blocks of organizations that have structurally equivalent positions in a network. Van de Ven, Walker, and Liston (1979) have successfully used block modeling techniques to analyze a network of 21 organizations that are members of a regional council for children and youth services in a middle-sized urban area in Texas. Taking a resource dependence framework, it was found that interorganizational clusters existed for three reasons: resource transactions, direct services, and planning and coordination. The responses given by agency personnel on the dimensions of IOR within each of the three major clusters were analyzed and comparisons drawn. The resource cluster of agencies reported the highest dependence upon each other and the highest formalization of agreements and contacts. The planning and coordination cluster reported the lowest dependence, the lowest formalization of agreements, and the most frequent use of committee meetings. The direct service cluster reported moderate amounts of dependence and formalized agreements and the least formalized agreements for contacting one another. This cluster reported the highest use of face-to-face contacts and telephone calls. The clusters of organizations in this service network were connected to one another by dominant agencies in the network (Van de Ven et al., 1979, pp. 31–35).

Some studies have used measures of the interorganizational structures of community that have not been based directly upon linkages between organizations. These few studies are very important because consequences (outputs) have also been determined in these studies. Mulford (1959) and Lorenz (1981) have used a combination of data obtained from mailed questionnaires sent to local officials and available census data to study the structure of business networks and local government, respectively.

Turk (1970; 1973; 1977) has been very creative in the development of measures of interorganizational networks for the 130 largest cities in the United States. The variables used in these studies and the results are reported in the next section.

Impact of Structure

The impact of interorganizational structures on organization sets and dyads has been observed in some empirical studies. For example, Whetten and Aldrich have sought to determine the organizational and environmental factors that most determine the size and composition of a social service agency's set of interorganizational linkages. The sets of 69 manpower organizations in New York were studied. A diverse organization set is thought to be functional in that alternative suppliers and customers may exist and diversity may increase a focal organization's ability to monitor the environment (1979, pp. 255–256). Based upon their results, Whetten and Aldrich conclude that set size and diversity are determined primarily by factors over which organization administrators have little control: the number of nonprofit organizations in the community; agency budget size; staff size, composition, and training; number and breadth of services offered; amount of boundary spanning; formalization of work rules; and frequency of staff meetings. In other words, the decisions made by federal and state program designers have a significant impact on the ability of local organizations to establish a large, and broadly based, network of relationships (pp. 268–275).

Consistent with the more general resource dependence model, Aiken and Hage (1968) have developed propositions about why organizations develop joint programs with other organizations. It is thought that program innovations lead to increased costs for organizations. Joint programs are thought to be developed in order to help pay for the costs of program innovation. Their research with health-related organizations provides support for the propositions. In an effort to evaluate the Aiken and Hage model in a comparative setting, Mulford (1981) has utilized data from a study of all voluntary organizations in three small communities in a Midwest county. Sociograms of exchanges and conflict reveal that the communities can be ordered from most environmental turbulence to least turbulence (see Chapter 3 for a review of environmental characteristics). After an analysis of available survey data and census data, it was concluded that these data also suggest that the communities can be ordered with regard to turbulence.

What affect does the interorganizatonal network have on the Aiken and Hage model? Are relationships moderated? Aiken and Hage's model is largely supported in the community with the least turbulence and only moderately supported in the community with more turbulence. In the community with more turbulence (relatively fewer exchange linkages and more conflict linkages), it was reported that program innovation on the part of an organization leads to conflict with other organizations and not to joint programs. It was concluded that innovations in a turbulent environment may be seen as threatening to other organizations.

A key concern has been to try to determine if interorganizational structure has an impact upon decisions made and activities implemented by communities. Three studies shed some light on this issue. Many small communities have sought to establish industrial development corporations in order to attract new industries and businesses. Mulford (1959) was interested in determining which small communities were most likely to establish development corporations. It was argued that communities that were the most integrated would be most able to promote this innovation and that communities that had experienced the least gains in retail sales over a decade would be most motivated. The number of organizations related to commerce and industry and the number of members were used as a measure of integration. A total of 27 small communities with development corporations were compared to a matched sample of 27 that did not have corporations in this study. The propositions were supported; communities with more integration and greater need were more likely to have adopted this innovation.

In his study of outputs from the 130 largest cities in the United States, Turk (1970) has proposed that integration among local units, extralocal integration, and need or demand may be related to the activity levels and complexity of new interorganizational networks. The proposition was specified and tested in terms of Turk's analysis of the flow of poverty funds from federal agencies to and among organizations in the cities. Integration among local units was measured by the incidence of community-wide civic associations and the degree of control by its municipal governments. Extralocal integration was measured by the number of national associational headquarters the city contained. Extralocal integration predicted the level of interorganizational activity best, and the measures of local integration predicted the complexity best. Need or demand, inferred from poverty rates and other forms of deprivation, made an impact only on such predictions where the levels of integration were high. In related research, Turk (1973) has found that the presence of community-wide voluntary associations and the scale and diversity of municipal government are positively related to the formation of hospital councils in cities.

After this study, Turk (1973, p. 37) concluded that the integrative significance of government and voluntary organizations may rest less upon linking persons to their environments than upon linking organizations to one another. In summary, Turk's research indicates that the activation of specific interorganizational networks depends directly upon the existing capacity for IOR and the demand that exists. Various kinds of demands compete with each other in cities until a demand around which the winning coalition of organizations can be formed emerges. Turk reasons that given the capacity and the demand for specific interorganizational networks, networks will occur. But he states that the mode of interorganizational activation is likely to be patterned by external standards (Turk, 1977, pp. 199–202).

Modeling his theory and measurement of variables closely after Turk, Lorenz (1981), in his recent study of 132 communities, has attempted to determine which community characteristics are related to a local government's utilization of regional councils of government technical assistance for planning, writing grants, and preparing surveys. Data were obtained through interviews with mayors and available census data were also used in the analysis. Lorenz (p. 98) reasoned that, if Turk's logic would hold, communities high on economic complexity, diversification of municipal government, political organization, and presence of voluntary organizations ought to have strong positive correlations between objective indicators of need and utilization of regional council technical assistance.

Lorenz (pp. 63–65) measured community need for resources with a variety of data including poverty rates, population over age 65, number of substandard housing units, and ratio of actual mill rate to statutory limit. Complexity and vertical linkages were measured by the number of corporations and the presence of extralocal corporations located in the community. Scale of local government was measured by the employees per capita and diversification by the number of position titles. The community's capacity to mediate conflict was also expected to be related to utilization of technical assistance and was measured by the presence of mayor-council forms of government and with elections by ward. Integration was measured by the number of voluntary organizations and by the number of daily or weekly newspapers present in a community.

The variables most highly correlated with utilization of technical assistance included number of extralocal corporations, diversification of local government, mayor-council government and elections by wards, number of voluntary organizations, and number of daily or weekly newspapers. Indicators of need for resources were poorly correlated with utilization (Lorenz, 1981, pp. 155–157). Contrary to Lorenz's expectations, the general pattern found was that given organizationally complex communities displaying systemic linkages, it is those communities with the least need for resources in terms of poverty rates, few elderly, and few substandard housing units that are most likely to utilize regional council technical assistance. It may be that communities with fewer resources can't afford to have municipal employees spend their time working with regional councils. In addition, communities with fewer resources may not be able to raise matching funds if grants are approved. Lorenz indicates that these results do provide support for the notion that community action in communities is organizationally based and most likely to occur in communities that display systemic properties (pp. 101–107).

One tentative conclusion that can be drawn from the studies reported in this section is that network integration makes collective decisions and action more feasible. A high priority is to find out more about processes in networks that promote integration. In particular, more studies of interorganizational coordination should be completed. Interorganizational coordination is a process in which organizatons jointly make decisions and/or act with regard to their shared task environment. What modes of coordination are possible? What are the costs and benefits of different modes of coordination?

Aiken and his colleagues (1975) have completed a series of case studies of alternative coordination strategies for the delivery of human services. The ideal strategy according to this study would include a coalition of organizations representing clients, professionals, and the community at large, with the coalition being funded collectively (pp. 170–178). Gans and Horton (1975) have completed a comparative analysis of 30 projects involving human services integration. Three modes of coordination were studied: voluntary, mediated, and directed coordination. With voluntary coordination, the integrator is responsible for the delivery of services and for development linkages with other service providers. With directed coordination, the integrator has the authority to mandate the development of linkages between legally subordinate organizations. With mediated coordination, the primary mission of the coordinator is the development of linkages between service providers (pp. 40). The impacts of the alternative modes of coordination were evaluated in terms of accessibility for clients, continuity of services, and efficiency.

Gans and Horton (pp. 5–13, 50–52) report that the amount of actual service integration is not extensive, and there is no one best services integration model. The kind of impact achieved appears to depend upon the mode of coordination used and the administrative and service linkage mechanisms developed. A wide variety of linkage mechanisms are discussed by Gans and Horton, a study highly recommended for both specialists and practitioners.

SUMMARY

We have seen that resource dependence theory and political economic theory, different from resource dependence primarily in terms of the importance it places on the function of external linkages, are the two major tools used to conceptualize networks of organizations. To this point, theorists have shown more concern for explaining how network linkages are formed and maintained than they have for the mechanisms through which partial or total networks are mobilized for collective action or for the actual production of collective decisions and actions. The empirical research is currently dominated by efforts to measure the structure of networks, locate subnetwork units, and account for the differential amounts of power that exist among organizations. A great deal of work does indeed remain to be done.

Unless specialists broaden their views and respond to these challenges, the promise of network analysis will not be realized. Network research can be quite expensive and time consuming, especially if longitudinal research is contemplated. Where are these resources to come from? Who will support this work? Theories about networks will continue to be incomplete until they are grounded in terms of real networks in the public and private sectors. Applied research on networks funded by public and private agencies and business should be encouraged because this research is most likely to be funded and because it shows great promise.

DISCUSSION QUESTIONS

1. What does the term "network" mean?
2. What can we learn from network studies that is not possible from studies of less comprehensive units?
3. What theoretical models are helpful in analyzing networks?

4. What are the relative advantages of loosely coupled networks? Give examples of loosely coupled networks in your community.

5. What are some of the most important resources thought to influence relationships in networks?

6. What are "interfirm organizations" and what can we learn from them about the mobilization of networks?

7. What factors encourage the development of coalitions?

8. What functions do graphs and matrices play in the analysis of networks?

9. What evidence do we have that the structure of networks has an impact on particular organizations and/or dyads?

10. How does network integration make collective decisions and action more feasible?

A CASE STUDY: PROPOSED, FEDERATIONS OF HUMAN SERVICE ORGANIZATIONS*

This *actual case* involves efforts by funders of 32 human service organizations in Story County, Iowa, to get the organizations to form five federations. It was proposed that funding bodies would allocate human service funding through the five service area administrations. The items presented here for your analysis consist of excerpts from news stories from a local newspaper, the *Ames Tribune*. All stories were written by Pat Kinney, *Tribune* staff writer.

January 9, 1981   Human Service Groups Proposed

In an effort to eliminate "unproductive competition" among Story County human service agencies and reduce their admin-

*Reprinted by permission from the *Ames Tribune,* Diane Pounds, News Editor; Pat Kinney, Writer.

istrative expenses, the study team has recommended those agencies be grouped into five federations. The Human Services Survey and Analysis Team made that recommendation in a 12-page report presented at its Thursday night meeting to about 30 human service representatives.

Currently there are 32 human service agencies in Story County, providing programs for youth and the elderly, child care, substance abuse treatment, and other services. Those agencies are funded by at least two of four funding bodies: the board of supervisors, the Ames City Council, the Ames-Gilbert United Way, or the Government of the Student Body at Iowa State University.

Within the federation proposed by the survey and analysis team, each existing human service agency would retain its autonomy, survey team members stressed. But the administrative work for each agency—including accounting and the search for financial assistance—would be done by one "service coordinator," giving each agency's staff more time for serving the community.

The five proposed federations are:

1. Health and Development—Ames Visiting Nurses; Homemaker Health Aides; Central Iowa Mental Health; Mainstream Living; Story County Developmental Center; Story County Center for Personal Development.

2. Child Care Services—Ames Community Pre-School; Cooperative Childcare Services; Edith Hale Childcare; Grace Grue Childcare; University Married Community Childcare; Community Health Support Services.

3. Community Services—YMCA; YWCA; Boys Club of Ames; Family Enrichment - The People Place; Legal Aid.

4. Senior Citizen Services—Ames Area Coordinating Committee for Senior Citizens; Colo Senior Citizens; Community Center (Aid to Independents); Kelley Senior Citizens; Nevada Senior Citizens; Council on Aging; Retired Senior Volunteer Program.

5. Crisis and Social Rehabilitation—Open Line; Story County Community Action; Sexual Assault Center and Battered Women's Project; Committee on Criminal Justice; Manpower; Regional Substance Abuse Center; Youth and Shelter Services.

Funding bodies would allocate human service funding through the five service area administrations to individual human service agencies, team members explained. Each service area coordinator would prepare a comprehensive plan for that area, including each human service agency. Presently, each agency prepares an individual budget and makes several presentations to each funding body.

Reactions from human service agency representatives Thursday ranged from favorable to skeptical. One representative told team members they had "done the impossible," while another said the team was proposing "another layer of bureaucracy." Several persons had questions on how the proposals would be brought about. "I'm scared to death" one representative said.

March 25, 1981   Groups Resent Plans

Many Ames and Story County human service agency personnel resent local government's plans for them, and local officials don't like their attitude.

The Ames City Council and Story County Board of Supervisors Tuesday heard comments from human service personnel on a reorganization plan for human service groups. The reorganization headline of next year (January budget sessions) may be flexible, city and county officials indicated.

The agencies' attitude toward the reorganization, and toward local government, has worsened. Some human service agencies resent their exclusion from the survey and analysis team's study and reorganization planning is still present.

"It appears that there is more distrust and apprehension now than even two months ago—distrust of the survey and analysis team of the funders and among human service agencies," the president of the Human Services Council said. She asked for more time to allow agencies "to strengthen relationships among ourselves" and look at alternatives. "This act has been interpreted by many to mean that the elected officials, who represent the public, are not meeting their responsibilities."

"Without cooperation it isn't going to work," a county supervisor said of the reorganization plan. "We hear the process is not going to work. If that is the case, maybe we're going to have to make some changes."

A representative of the Ames-Gilbert United Way, praised the survey and analysis team's work but questioned their plan. He noted some agency workers are concerned about losing their autonomy through reorganization. There is concern "the curtailment of their responsibilities will lead to the curtailment of their enthusiasm and involvement," he said.

The survey and analysis team chairman said the reorganization isn't designed so agencies will have to surrender autonomy to a federation director. The plan is not another layer of bureaucracy, he said, rebutting arguments made by some agency representatives.

A city council member suggested local funds may be allocated more equitably through the federations. She said human service funding now often comes down to "who speaks the best at the microphone" as each individual agency makes its pitch.

March 29, 1981   United Way Cool to Plan

The Ames-Gilbert United Way has declined to participate in a plan to reorganize Story County human service agencies.

In its letter, the United Way board of directors wrote, "So far, the United Way has not been able to determine what the costs of the proposed federation would be either in short or long term; nor can it learn what cost efficiencies would result from this federation." But the cost of reorganization, and actual cost savings of the proposed reorganization, are unknown, the United Way board of directors said. "These two very important questions continue to be unanswered, along with others that make it almost impossible to determine what the currently proposed plan . . . can better accomplish for human service in Story County."

The survey team leader responded to the letter by saying many of the questions the United Way has will be answered as the reorganization planning continues. He said the survey team will keep the United Way informed of the planning process, and probably will submit items to the United Way for approval when the planning is completed. The United Way funds 28 of the 32 human service agencies and raises about $250,000 for them annually.

April 3, 1981   Service Teams to Reorganize Selves

The Human Service Survey and Analysis Team is trying to improve its relations with human service agencies as they work toward reorganization.

The team will be leaving the reorganization efforts up to the agencies. But the human services team will be available for help if needed.

"The impetus is no longer on us but on them (human service agencies)," the team chairman said at a team meeting this week. "We're willing to work with them."

The team sent letters to each agency this week, indicating survey and analysis team members will be available to assist agencies in their reorganization. Team members will be representatives of the city of Ames and Story County, two of the local bodies funding human service groups.

The letters to each agency ask whether the agency is satisfied with its placement in a particular federation. Some agencies have asked to be transferred to another federation, and asked that federations be renamed.

The goals of the management team will be to simplify each federation's efforts in securing financial aid from the four local funding bodies—Ames, Story County, the Ames-Gilbert United Way and Iowa State's Government of the Student Body.

The team will attempt to design a single accounting form used by all local funders in determining funding for each human service federation. The team hopes to have funding decisions made at a single hearing, at which all local funders will be present.

Currently, each human service agency must make funding requests at separate hearings of each funding body.

A member of the Human Services Council said he thinks the survey and analysis team will improve relations with human service groups by letting them know it is willing to work with them and wants their participation in the reorganization plan.

July 23, 1981   Agencies Cautious

Apparently 32 local human service agencies are cooperating cautiously in a reorganization mandated by Ames and Story County officials.

Although they're cooperating, some agency representatives still are concerned about what might happen to their agencies, and the people they serve.

Human service agency representatives listened without comment as a report on their reorganization was presented to the Ames City Council and the Story County Board of Supervisors Tuesday by the chair of the Human Services Survey and Analysis Team. That team proposed the reorganization in December, after a nine-month study.

The meeting was much quieter than a human services forum held March 24, during which human service agencies expressed strong reservations and opposition to the plan.

City and county officials asked for the agencies' cooperation, and they're apparently getting it now, even though some resistance to and pessimism about the reorganization still exists.

The proposed federations have met, designated spokespersons, and are organizing, the council and supervisors were told by the chair.

But the chair also noted several unresolved questions. One major issue is whether governmental bodies should allocate human service funds directly to the agencies, or through the federations.

One alternative suggested is that agencies be funded directly for the coming year, with funding by federation to begin in 1983. The final decision will be up to the governmental bodies.

Another major issue is a proposed human services conference to be held each mid-January. Those conferences, previously held in the fall, mainly concentrated on distribution of annual funding. But long-range agency programs also may be discussed at the new conferences.

At Tuesday night's meeting, a Story County Supervisor said

agencies often in competition for funds already have benefited from the reorganization process, because they're more aware of related agencies' operations than before.

October 8, 1981   Services Funding Decided

A Story County Supervisor called it a transition step. An Ames City Council member said it was a step backward.

Those were some of the comments as the city council and the Story County Board of Supervisors Tuesday night aproved a method on how to fund child care, senior citizen programs, substance abuse treatment, youth and other human services agencies for fiscal year 1982–83.

Council members and the supervisors agreed to fund human services "by federation, with agency designation," as the council and supervisors decide how to fund human services for 1982–83, they will review budget forms for five human service federations, with the budget for 32 individual human service agencies also designated on those forms. Funds will be allocated to the agencies, not the federations.

Ultimately, the council and supervisors want to be able to review five human service budgets, instead of 32. They are concerned that federal budget cuts will mean they will have less money to distribute to human service groups.

However, council members' and supervisors' one-year timetable for human service reorganization apparently will not be met. Human service agencies are not ready to be funded by federations for the next fiscal year, 1982–83.

Under the compromise proposal which the council and supervisors ultimately approved, "we consider federations, but allocate funds to individual agencies."

One council member said preparing federation budgets and allocating funds to individual agencies would be a "shell game. We shouldn't fool ourselves into thinking we are giving the federations any viability."

Another council member said, "I take it as one step toward an ultimate goal, and the agencies do too. Some human beings are involved," he said, referring to the human service workers going through the reorganization. He said progress has been made "by the very impact" of the reorganization, which has forced agencies to sit down together. And they're talking about a step further—consolidation."

At a human services council meeting which he attended last month, some agency representatives said that the proposed federations actually would lead to the consolidation of human service agencies.

The council member who cast the lone dissenting vote as the council and supervisors approved the funding proprosal indicated he feels human services agencies should be funded as they have been in previous years.

"I don't think I can vote for funding for anything other than by agency, because I don't know how far along the federations are," he said. "I don't know that the federations exist."

QUESTIONS FOR DISCUSSION

1. Which organizational, dyadic, and system properties can you see at work in this case?

2. Which theoretical model seems to be most helpful in analyzing the case, e.g., the resource exchange, resource dependence, or political economic model?

3. What do you think will be the results of these efforts by the funders?

REFERENCES

Aiken, M., Dewar, R., DiTomaso, N., Hage, J., & Zeitz, G. *Coordinating human services*. San Francisco: Jossey-Bass, 1975.

Aiken, M., & Hage, J. Organizational interdependence and intraorganizational structure. *American Sociological Review*, 1968, *33*, 912–930.

Aldrich, H. E. An organization-environment perspective on cooperaton and conflict between organizations in the manpower training system. In A. R. Negandhi (Ed.), *Conflict and power in complex organizations: An interinstitutional perspective*. Kent, OH: Kent State University Press, 1972, pp. 11–38.

————An interorganizational dependency perspective on relations between the employment service and its organization-set. In R. H. Killman, L. R. Pondy, & D. P. Slevin (Ed.), *The management of organizational design, Vol. III.* New York: Elsevier North-Holland, 1976, pp. 231–266.

————*Organizations and environments.* Englewood Cliffs, NJ: Prentice-Hall, 1979.

Benson, J. K. The interorganizational network as a political economy. *Administrative Science Quarterly,* 1975, *20,* 229–249.

Child, J. Organization structure, environment, and performance—the role of strategic choice. *Sociology,* 1972, *6,* 1–22.

Clark, T. N. Citizen values, power, and policy outputs: A model of community decision-making. *Journal of Comparative Administration,* 1973, *4,* 385–427.

Evan, W. M. Toward of theory of interorganizational relations. *Management Science,* 1965, *11,* 217–231.

Galaskiewicz, J. The structure of community organizational networks. *Social Forces,* 1979, *57,* 1346–1364.

Gans, S. P., & Horton, G. T. *Integration of Human Services.* New York: Praeger, 1975.

Laumann, E. O., & Pappi, F. H. *Networks of collective action.* New York: Academic Press, 1976.

Laumann, E. O., Galaskiewicz, J., & Marsden, P. V. Community structure as interorganizational linkages. *Annual Review of Sociology.* Palo Alto, CA: Annual Reviews Inc., 1978, pp. 455–483.

Lorenz, F. O. *City utilization of regional council technical assistance.* Unpublished Ph.D. dissertation, Iowa State University, Ames, IA, 1981.

Mitchell, J. C. The concept and use of social networks. In J. C. Mitchell (Ed.), *Social networks in urban situations.* Manchester, England: Manchester University Press, 1969, pp. 1–50.

Mulford, C. L. *Relation between community variables and local industrial development corporations.* Unpublished M.S. thesis, Iowa State University, Ames, IA, 1959.

————*Some relationships between formal organizations, community problems, and leadership.* Unpublished Ph.D. dissertation, Iowa State University, Ames, IA. 1962.

————*Interdependence and intraorganizational structure in three communities.* Unpublished paper, Iowa State University, Ames, IA, 1981.

Perrucci, R., & Pilisuk, M. Leaders and ruling elites: The interorganizational bases of community power. *American Sociological Review,* 1970, *35,* 1040–1057.

Pfeffer, J., & Salancik, G. R. *The external control of organizations.* New York: Harper and Row, 1978.

Phillips, A. A theory of interfirm organizations. *Quarterly Journal of Economics,* 1960, *74,* 602–613.

Rubin, J. Z, & Brown, B. R. *The social psychology of bargaining and negotiation.* New York: Academic Press, 1975.

Tichy, N., & Fombrun, C. Network analysis in organizational settings. *Human Relations,* 1979, *32,* 923–965.

Turk, H. Comparative urban studies in interorganizational relations. *Sociological Inquiry,* 1969, *38,* 108–110.

Turk, H. Interorganizational networks in urban society: Initial perspectives and comparative research. *American Sociological Review,* 1970, *35,* 1–19.

————Comparative urban structure from an interorganizational perspective. *Administrative Science Quarterly,* 1973, *18,* 37–55.

————*Organizations in modern life.* San Francisco: Jossey-Bass, 1977.

Van de Ven, A. H. *Assessing organizations.* New York: John Wiley and Sons, 1980.

Van de Ven, A. H., Walker, G., & Liston, J. Coordination patterns within an interorganizational network. *Human Relations,* 1979, *32,* 19–36.

Warren, R. L. The interorganizational field as a focus for investigation. *Administrative Science Quarterly,* 1967, *12,* 396–419.

Warren, R. L., Bergunder, A. F., Newton, J. W., & Rose, S. M. The interaction of community decision organizations: Some conceptual considerations and empirical findings. In A. R. Negandhi (Ed.), *Interorganization theory.* Kent, OH: Kent State University Press, 1975, pp. 167–181.

Whetten, D. A., & Aldrich, H. E. Organization set size and diversity. *Administration and Society,* 1979, *11,* 251–281.

Williamson, O. E. A dynamic theory of interfirm behavior. *Quarterly Journal of Economics,* 1965, *79,* 579–607.

Yuchtman, E., & Seashore, S. E. A system resource approach to organizational effectiveness. *American Sociological Review,* 1967, *32,* 891–903.

Zald, M. Political economy: A framework for comparative analysis. In M. Zald (Ed.), *Power in organizations.* Nashville, TN: Vanderbilt University Press, 1970.

Chapter 7

CONTRIBUTIONS TO COMMUNITY
DEVELOPMENT

Concern is expressed today by persons in many walks of life that something is wrong with the community, that community problems exist. The purpose of this chapter is to show some of the ways in which an interorganizational perspective is helpful when thinking about community development. Community problems themselves, and strategies for alleviating these problems, have been discussed in terms of the community's vertical and horizontal patterns. A community's vertical pattern has to do with relationships between community units and extracommunity systems and often involves different hierarchical levels. It is commonly lamented that communities, or units within them, have lost their autonomy and power relative to state or federal levels. Indeed, community development has been defined by Warren as "*a deliberate and sustained attempt to strengthen the horizontal pattern of a community*" (Warren, 1978, pp. 324–325). The obsolescence of some rural communities has been described in terms of their inability to function effectively and to provide services for residents. For example, the U.S. National Advisory Commission on Rural Poverty (1967) has emphatically recommended that regional and area-wide social structures should be

171

created and coordinated on a state and national basis in order to combat the decline in rural communities and promote collective decision making.

Persons who have been concerned about the delivery of human services see community problems in terms of inadequate coordination between program funders and service providers and call for appropriate linkage mechanisms (for example see Aiken, Dewar, Di Tomaso, Hage, and Zeitz, 1975; Gans and Horton, 1975). Communities that make greater use of Regional Council of Government assistance in grant writing, surveys, and planning have been described in terms of the linkage complexity in the public and private sectors (Lorenz, 1981). In addition, the capacity for needed interorganizational networks in large cities in the United States is thought to be primarily dependent upon the availability of local linkages that enable coalitions to develop and upon the development of external linkages (Turk, 1977).

The perspective that sees community development in terms of a strengthened horizontal pattern, the call for greater regionalization and area-wide structures to help develop rural communities, concerns about existing delivery systems, and interest in the activation of networks in large cities have one key element in common. Each concern recognizes the important role of organizations in communities and each emphasizes the development or strengthening of appropriate linkages between organizations.

Whether or not an interorganizational perspective on community development will be widely adopted remains to be seen. Three questions must be answered affirmatively before this perspective on community development can prove fruitful. First, is the existing knowledge base really relevant for persons with community development interests? Applied persons interested in community development need to know how to improve the operation of organizations and how reluctant organizations can be influenced to participate in development projects, about factors that facilitate or retard dyadic relationships, and about alternative ways in which coordination can be accomplished in networks. Some of the research that has been completed seems especially relevant with regard to these needs, and highlights of the work will be discussed in this chapter. Even if the knowledge base does show potential, have specialists been motivated to develop guidelines, games, simulation exercises, or other training materials? A small number of prototype guides for practitioners, some even with specific action steps to be followed, have been developed. The characteristics of these guides will be discussed and their relative merits evaluated. Finally, it should be asked, even if the knowledge base is judged sufficient, and even if some training materials have been developed, are the materials being used? Are persons with community development interests being trained? The answer to this last question is at most a very weak and tentative yes. Some of the reasons for this lack of utilization will be presented in this chapter and suggestions made for improving training.

DEVELOPMENT INTERVENTIONS WITH ORGANIZATIONS, DYADS, AND NETWORKS

Not only do options exist with regard to the point of intervention for community development but other options also exist with regard to the kinds of interventions possible. For some community development work it may be necessary to intervene at more than one point and employ several strategies. The goal may be to help particular organizations develop joint projects to better meet the needs of their clients or more effectively monitor their environment; the goal may be to encourage particular dyadic relationships. Alternately, the goal may be to intervene at the network level or to create an entirely new network and hope to affect relationships on a comprehensive scale.

Influencing the Linkages Developed by Particular Organizations

Let's suppose first that a community development practitioner wishes to know which organizations are most likely to be willing to participate in joint projects. We already know a considerable bit about the characteristics of particular organizations that are more likely to develop linkages with others, although we know much less about the impact of the relationships on the structure and functioning of the organizations. Organizations that have participated in previous joint projects are more likely than others to participate again. Although some organizations with insufficient resources may be willing to participate in a joint community project to help defray costs they could not bear alone, research indicates that human service organizations and voluntary organizations with relatively more resources than others are most likely to participate. We know too that human service organizations and voluntary organizations that are larger and already sponsor a greater number of activities for the community are more complex; they are more innovative and more likely to participate in joint projects. We also know that organizations will develop contacts with other organizations, exchange information, and place members on each other's boards in order to reduce environmental uncertainty and aid their decision making (see Chapter 3 for a view of environmental strategies).

In summary, organizations respond to their environment (including other organizations) at least partly in order to reduce uncertainty and because of resource dependency or to position other organizations into a state of dependency. That some organizations find it necessary to interact with other organizations has a double-edged meaning from an applied point of view.

Pfeffer and Salancik (1978) have observed that organizations in a state of dependency either comply with the demands of others or they act in various ways to manage the dependencies that create constraints on organizational activities. First, community development practitioners interested in improving the operations of organizations that are at least partly externally controlled may find it to their advantage to help organization decision makers think about the appropriate design of these organizations. Second, one of the most effective ways to directly influence particular organizations is to manipulate the context in which they operate. Others have also commented upon prescriptive models of organizations (for example, see Nystrom and Starbuck, 1977), but the recent book by Pfeffer and Salancik provides an in-depth analysis. Four implications of the resource dependence perspective for better organizational design are discussed by Pfeffer and Salancik:

1. designs for effective environmental scanning systems,
2. designs for loosening dependencies on other organizations,
3. designs for managing conflicting demands and constraints,
4. designs of chief executive positions.

Organizations that have lost touch with their environment or face changing and uncertain environments may find it necessary to make certain that some persons are specifically charged with the responsibility of scanning the environment. Organizations with sufficient resources may find it possible to establish a scanning unit or units. In addition, communication blocks must be eliminated within the organization and steps taken to make certain that decision makers will effectively use information possessed by all relevant persons for planning. It may be the desire of the community development practitioner to help a particular organization increase its autonomy and loosen its dependencies on others. Diversification is one of the most important tactics that can be used to loosen dependencies on other organizations. Organizations with many recipients of their services or products are less controlled than those with a few suppliers or recipients of their services or products. When an organization disperses its dependency among numerous organizations, it may be necessary to differentiate and establish subunits to deal with homogeneous subsegments of its environment. Differentiation allows for the satisfaction of different, and perhaps conflicting, demands at the same time. In addition, diversification reduces the necessity of the organization's need to respond to any particular demand. Finally, it may be functional for decision-making power to be decentralized in some organizations that are externally controlled or to insure that executives can easily be removed when environmental conditions require new leadership.

Pfeffer and Salancik (1978) indicate that the profoundly important topic of designing organizational environments as a strategy to induce changes in organizations has been largely ignored. The appropriate design of environments depends upon what interests are to be served. One can easily see the impact of economic policies and regulations established (or deregulation) by government on organizations in the private sector. Changes in funding procedures, policies, and regulations can also be used to directly influence the context within which human service and other public sector organizations operate. For example, when funders of human service organizations require that planning for and delivery of human service programs occur on a county- or area-wide basis, organizations are forced to interact in order to obtain funds (Pfeffer and Salancik, pp. 268–281).

Influencing Dyads of Organizations

Sometimes, in the interest of community development, it may be necessary to get particular organizations to relate to each other. Researchers and persons with applied interests have made efforts to identify factors that inhibit or facilitate the development of relationships between specific organizations in dyads. Lauffer (1978, pp. 214–218), writing from his experience with social planning in the human services, has specified seven factors that he thinks can be used to overcome resistance. These factors include:

1. the capability of the planner;
2. availability of fiscal and related resources;
3. public and environmental support;
4. complementary organizational functions;
5. the existence of a support system, including standardized data collection procedures that will improve communication—communication maintained through task forces or consumer groups and the physical proximity of some organizations;
6. idiosyncratic factors such as the results of previous interaction; and

7.   the existence of self-help organizations advocating on their own behalf.

Schermerhorn (1975) has conducted an analysis of the general literature on cooperation between organizations and has developed a set of determinants of interorganizational cooperation. Schermerhorn has concluded that the major motivators include:

1.   resource scarcity or performance distress,
2.   the existence of values that stress cooperation as a good thing to be doing, and
3.   powerful extraorganizational forces that demand cooperation.

Barriers to cooperation include:

1.   a fear of loss of autonomy,
2.   fears that organizational participation will have unfavorable ramifications for image or identity, and
3.   fears that participation will require the direct expenditure of scarce resources.

A number of empirical studies of dyadic interaction have been conducted in recent years and these results may be helpful when practitioners think about factors that might facilitate or impede interaction between particular organizations. A review of the empirical literature (see Chapter 4) has identified several comparative properties associated with exchanges of resources and conflict between organizations in dyads. However, some of these comparative properties are nearly impossible to manipulate directly. For example, it has been found that organizations that accept each other's domain as legitimate, have goals that are similar, and adminstrators comparable in social status, are more likely to exchange a variety of resources with each other.

Specific comparative properties may be difficult to change or manipulate. It may be easier to manipulate or influence other important comparative properties in order to encourage exchanges. For example, frequency of contact between organizations, scarcity of resources, and perceived mutual dependence are comparative properties that make resource exchange more likely. Efforts could be made to encourage contacts between organizations. Resources might be offered contingent upon the organizations' joint participation. Sometimes organizations are not aware of the extent of their interdependence. Perhaps they have common clients, provide comparable programs, or obtain funds from the same sources. These interdependencies can be emphasized. In addition, their mutual dependencies can be increased through mandates or procedures established by funders. For example, funders might require that particular organizations will make joint budget requests to them, plan a joint program, or use the same administrative support staff.

Influencing Networks of Interaction

Practitioners realize that it is sometimes necessary to encourage increased IOR for particular organizations and dyadic interaction between particular organizations. In addition, it is sometimes necessary to use comprehensive strategies in order to influence the operation of whole networks. Benson (1975) has provided considerable insight in his discussion of networks as political economies. External agencies, interest groups, and funders, through their manipulation of key resources (money and authority), can have a direct influence on whole networks of service providers. Although Benson wasn't necessarily writing for applied audiences specifically, his insights are keen and this study is highly recommended.

Lauffer (1978, pp. 223–236) has described comprehensive coordinating mechanisms that have been used to try to increase coordination in the human services at the local level. These mechanisms became prominent during the 1970s:

1. the transfer of authority for policy and planning from the federal level,
2. functional consideration of both special district and general-purpose local governments, and

3. the creation of programmatic and administrative mechanisms for planning and coordination in area-wide and local services.

Revenue sharing represents one very specific effort to transfer authority to state and local governments. When regulations governing revenue sharing require that public involvement occur when decisions are made about the allocation of funds, various organizations involving clients and professionals are forced to interact. When general revenue-sharing funds are allocated to states or local governments, organizations from competing networks interact to set funding priorities. Substate districts or area-wide coordinating bodies such as regional councils, metropolitan planning commissions, and other regional program administrations are frequently developed in order to promote coordination within networks. Unfortunately, the areas served by various coordinating bodies do not always coincide and citizens and professional planners are sometimes faced with confusion. Mechanisms which allow designated area-wide agencies to review the adequacy of and comment upon (to "sign off") proposals for grants made by local government organizations within an area, are important because federal agencies take these recommendations into consideration when granting funds.

Very valuable descriptive studies of alternative coordination models have been completed. Aiken and his colleagues (1975) have completed an analysis of coordination of services for the mentally retarded in five metropolitan areas in the United States. In order to establish an appropriate structure of coordination, one that assumes the representation of diverse interests, three units may be needed, namely, a unit to do case coordination, a coalition of organizations, and a community board. Case coordination is stressed because it meets the needs of clients better than when each organization works independently with the mentally retarded. Coalitions of organizations that are funded collectively may reduce competition and fears about losses of autonomy that result when funds go to a single organization. The community board is intended to protect the public interest (Aiken et al., 1975, pp. 170–174).

Options exist with regard to the elements that are actually coordinated. At least four kinds of elements can be coordinated: resources, programs and program development, clients, and communication. Coordination of all elements may not be possible or even desirable. However, a plan that does not specifically consider all four elements will not result in a fully integrated delivery system. Once the elements for coordination have been determined, decisions should be reached regarding how they will be coordinated. Certain elements generally can best be coordinated at specific levels (see Figure 7-1). Coordination of resources, i.e., joint decisions as to which organizations will get which resources, is thought to be best conducted by representatives at the broad, community-wide, institutional level. For example, fund raising in many communities is done through the United Way. However, coordination with regard to programs, program development,

Figure 7-1. Elements to Coordinate and Appropriate Levels.
[Adapted from Aiken et al. (1975, 10–17.]

Elements	Levels
Resources ⟶	Community-Wide Institutional Level
Programs ⟶	Organizational Decision-Maker Level
Clients ⟶	Agency Line Staff
Information ⟶	All Levels

and the avoidance of duplicate programs may best be done by relevant agency decision makers when they are motivated to do so. Program coordination is often aided by informal relationships among professionals.

Those who work most closely with the clients, or people who receive the benefits from the organizations, can do the best job of coordination that directly involves the clients. Information should be coordinated at all levels. Information relevant to the coordination project should flow freely between all participants. Those who need to know should know. For example, in university extension programs, county and area administrators and state program leaders know if funds are available for new programs. These administrators are trained in program development and are also knowledgeable about programs provided by other educational agencies.

Aiken and his colleagues have also specified the major barriers that they think impede coordination in mental retardation networks. These barriers include a fear of loss of autonomy, different professional ideologies, and attemps by interest groups to dominate the network. When different values are held by resource controllers at different levels of government, coordination is made more difficult. Finally, the presence of multiple units of local government in metropolitan areas also impedes coordination. Coordination is nearly impossible when too many units of government or governmental agencies are involved (Aiken et al, 1975, pp. 10–124).

Gans and Horton (1975) have completed an intensive analysis of three contrasting models of coordination used to deliver a variety of human services in 30 cities and provide many very interesting ideas and insights for those with community development interests. Those three models of coordination studied in the 30 cities included voluntary, mediated, and directed coordination (see Figure 7-2). The "integrator" refers to the organizational entity (board, staff, or person) charged with coordinating the services of autonomous organizations. With voluntary coordination, the integrator provides services and also tries to encourage coordination. With mediated coordination, the integrator is charged with the development of linkages between

Figure 7-2. Three Models of Coordination. [Adapted from Gans and Horton (1975, 11–14).]

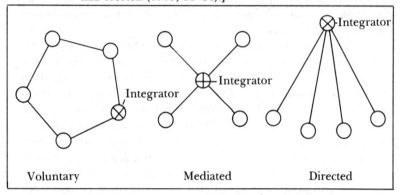

providers. When directed coordination is used, the integrator has the authority to mandate the development of linkages. Which model of coordination is best? Gans and Horton (1975, pp. 11–40) conclude that there is no one best services integration model. Rather, the three models tend to have different kinds of impact. This is a very important point. More clients receive services than before when voluntary coordination occurs and the clients are aided through the provision of multiple services. Mediated coordination helps to reduce service duplication and to standardize delivery procedures. Directed coordination holds promise for the development of a better planning capability to assess needs and resources, eliminating overlap and duplication and filling service gaps (Gans and Horton, pp. 11–14).

Linkages are the actual mechanisms used to establish coordination. A wide variety of linkages and their impact have been described by Gans and Horton (pp. 37–39; 91–93). Two categories of linkages were analyzed: administrative and direct service. Administrative linkages include fiscal linkages, such as joint budgeting, joint funding, and purchase of services; personnel practices, such as consolidated personnel administration; joint use of staff, staff transfers, and colocation of staff; program and planning; and administrative support services. Direct service linkages include core services, such as outreach, intake, and referrals, and modes of case coordination.

Some linkages take longer to develop because the autonomy of organizations is threatened but have high impact, e.g., joint budgeting, joint planning, and staff transfer. Other linkages take less time to develop but have less impact, e.g., purchase of services, joint training of staff, and information sharing (Gans and Horton, p. 16). And, as we might expect, some linkages are used more often with one model of coordination than with others. For example, joint budgeting is used less frequently with voluntary coordination. Joint use of staff, joint planning, and joint record keeping are also used less frequently with voluntary coordination. Direct service linkages are used with voluntary coordination and mediated coordination but not with directed coordination (Gans and Horton, pp. 91–93).

Gans and Horton (pp. 70–84) have provided us with a list of the major facilitators of coordination found in their analysis of the 30 projects and the major barriers to coordination. The major facilitating factors were positive support from the external sociopolitical environment in which the projects operated, a cooperative environment between the integrator and the service providers, and the positive effect that resulted when organizations did not unduly lose autonomy or lose control. The major barriers to coordination included negative attitudes on the part of the integrator and negative attitudes of funding sources toward changes in the delivery system. The negative factor that served as the major barrier to coordination was the desire of service providers to maintain agency prerogatives and control over the delivery of services. For some projects, service providers' independent influence with funders served as an additional barrier in that agency autonomy was reinforced and the perceived need to coordinate lessened. Finally, for some projects, service providers' thinking that they really were not part of a service delivery system served as a barrier to coordination.

Warren (1967, pp. 417–419) has considered ways in which the joint decision making of community decision organizations (CDOs) in cities might be improved. The issue is, short of centralization, are there linkages or procedures that might lead CDOs to have more comprehensive knowledge of each others' plans, policies, and programs? Warren suggests that the development of common data banks might be helpful, and he suggests that prompt communication about proposed policy or program changes should be considered. Other linkages to improve understanding include the exchange of board members and encouraging staff at various levels in CDOs to communicate with their counterparts. Joint planning between CDOs is suggested too. Finally, Warren adds that efforts should be made to establish central decision making to break impasses or resolve conflict and to improve the process of resource allocation among CDOs when the existing mix is seen as less than desirable.

GUIDELINES, CHECKLISTS, AND TRAINING MATERIALS FOR PRACTITIONERS

We have seen that the knowledge base shows promise and is relevant for some aspects of community development. Because researchers do not usually write with the needs of applied audiences in mind, articles in scientific journals and research monographs are seldom used directly by community development specialists. There is a definite need for persons to concisely summarize research results and develop guidelines, checklists, and materials that can be used in training. Have these materials been created for community specialists? An affirmative answer can be given if we mean materials to orient practitioners to the potential role IOR can play in community development. We will note in the next section that most of the existing materials provide only an orientation and not an in-depth analysis to the subject, and most training sessions are only a few hours in duration. The increasing number of applied materials being created is, however, a positive indication that the subject matter is judged relevant.

To illustrate the diversity of applied materials that exist for training, or that practitioners could use directly and benefit, three complementary items will be briefly discussed here: Lauffer's (1978, pp. 309–325) Interagency Cooperation Game, Whetten's (1977) guidelines for determining the degree of coordination possible, and Mulford and Klonglan's (1979) guide for creating and encouraging coordination, provide different training functions and could be used in conjunction with each other.

The Interagency "Cooperation Game" developed by Lauffer (pp. 309–325) is a most interesting training device. Roles played during the game include funders, various community influentials, agency personnel, consumers of services, and representatives of civic organizations. Participants must decide which community objectives are most important and attempt to get funds for proposed programs. Coalition formation is permissible. Project proposals are prepared, submitted for funding, and reviewed by funders during the course of the game. Can you think of a situation in which you could use the Lauffer game to stimulate greater interest in IOR?

Whetten (1977) has identified for practitioners three contextual factors that can strongly influence the likelihood of successful coordination, namely, the compatibility of organizations to be coordinated, the present availability of resources for the organizations, and the point at which the initiative for coordination develops, e.g., at the local level or at higher levels. Whetten is trying to help planners determine the degree of coordination possible. That is, Whetten states that the key to successful planning is to match the characteristics of each context with the appropriate level of coordination. For example, if the organizations are not very compatible, if they already have access to sufficient resources, and if the initiative for coordination comes from higher levels, little coordination is likely. Whetten's contingency approach to designing coordinated systems is unique in that he proposes that the "goodness of fit" between the level of coordination achieved and the contextual conditions present should be one of the principal criteria used when evaluating coordination efforts.

Mulford and Klonglan (1979) have developed an orientation and planning guide to help a variety of practitioners create coordination among organizations. An overview of models of coordination and linkage mechanisms is presented and common barriers and facilitators discussed and illustrated. A model consisting of 10 planning steps thought to be necessary for coordination is presented. Planning worksheets are included and can be used in workshops or by persons working alone. Workshop participants use the planning guide in small groups to design a real or hypothetical coordinated effort. This is one of the few planning models that specifically includes evaluation as a planning step. Other planning models with specific planning steps have been developed by Morris (1963), Aiken et al. (1975), Davidson (1976), and Fisher and Brown (1977).

Whetten's (1977) contingency model and Mulford and Klonglan's (1979) planning model can be used to plan real or hypothetical projects that require coordination between organizations and agencies. Or, these models might be used to evaluate a successful or unsuccessful coordinated effort with which you are familiar. For example, were contextual factors ignored? Were important planning steps skipped? Cases for analysis have been placed at the end of relevant chapters in this book. For practice, these planning models could be used to evaluate the contextual factors discussed in the cases for Chapters 4 and 6 and to begin thinking about what important steps would need to be taken in order for coordination to occur.

WHO GETS TRAINED ABOUT COORDINATION?

With the exception of Klonglan, Mulford, Warren, and Winklepleck (1975), who have developed a series of training options that range from short orientations for persons unacquainted with coordination as a concept to extended seminars of three days in length for experienced coordinators, most of the available training materials are only designed to provide an orientation to the topic of coordination or to stimulate thinking about coordination.

Training for coordination will be less effective when isolated individuals from particular agencies or communities attend, when the training is held in nonwork settings, and when no formal evaluation of training impact occurs. It is also quite unrealistic to expect short workshops to have great impact for community development. Unfortunately, most workshops on coordination have these negative characteristics.

There is a great need for intensive training about IOR to be included in the formal training of community development professionals. Positive steps are being taken. For example, community organization and planning texts increasingly contain material on IOR (e.g., see Cox, Erlich, Rothman, and Tropman, 1977; Kramer and Specht, 1975; Lauffer, 1978). The United States Department of Agriculture, Science and Education Administration used copies of the planning model developed by Mulford and Klonglan (1979) in a circuit riders packet for national distribution during 1981. "Circuit riders" are trained community development professionals who work for and with officials of participating small communities in order to help these communities improve their ability to deal with problems (Lovan, 1980). But much more needs to be done. Hopefully, researchers and community development professionals will be motivated during the years to come to do more of the work that is required for us to be able to measure the true value of this information for community development.

DISCUSSION QUESTIONS

1. How do ineffective linkages between organizations stand in the way of resolving social problems? Can you think of examples in your community?

2. What is unique about Warren's definition of community development?

3. What alternatives exist in terms of IOR intervention points?

4. How can a practitioner's knowledge about organization-environment interaction be helpful when consulting with particular organizations?

5. How can the design of organizational environments be used to help encourage the development of linkages between programs?

6. How can an understanding of comparative organizational properties be helpful for understanding how to encourage linkages between organizations?

7. Which linkages for promoting coordination are easiest to establish; which take the longest; and which linkages have the greatest impact?

8. How should one decide which model of coordination to use (voluntary, mediated, and directed)?

9. What kinds of barriers impede coordinated efforts?

10. What is your evaluation of the training on coordination currently available for practitioners? What are some top training priorities?

REFERENCES

Aiken, M., Dewar, R., Di Tomaso, N., Hage, J. & Zeitz, G. *Coordinating human services.* San Francisco: Jossey-Bass, 1975.

Benson, J. K. The interorganizational network as a political economy. *Administrative Science Quarterly*, 1975, *20*, 229–249.

Cox, F. M., Erlich, J. L., Rothman, J., & Tropman, J. E. *Tactics and techniques of community practice.* Itasca, Il: F. E. Peacock, 1977.

Davidson, S. M. Coordinating of social services in multiorganizational contexts. *Social Service Review*, 1976, *21*, 117–137.

Fisher, V. D., & Brown, F. G. *Interjurisdictional policy makers workshop.* Storrs, Connecticut: University of Connecticut, Institute of Public Service. August, 1977.

Gans, S. P., & Horton, G. T. *Integration of human services.* New York: Praeger, 1975.

Klonglan, G. E., Mulford, C. L., Warren R. D., & Winklepleck, J. M. *Creating Interorganizational Coordination: Project Report.* Department of Sociology, Iowa State University, Ames, IA: Sociology Report No. 122A, 1975. [This volume is one of a four-part series: 122B is an orientation to coordination, 122C is an instructor's guide, and 122D is a student's workbook.]

Kramer, R. M., & Specht, H. *Readings in community organization practice.* Englewood Cliffs: NJ: Prentice-Hall, 1975.

Lauffer, A. *Social planning at the community level.* Englewood Cliffs, NJ: Prentice-Hall, 1978.

Lorenz, F. O. *City utilization of regional council technical assistance.* Iowa State University, Ames, Iowa, Unpublished Ph.D. dissertation, 1981.

Lovan, R. W. Personal communication by letter. Washington, DC: United States Department of Agriculture, Science and Education Administration, September 26, 1980.

Morris, R. Basic factors in planning for the coordination of health services. *American Journal of Public Health,* 1963, *53,* 248–259, 462–472.

Mulford, C. L., & Klonglan, G. E. Creating coordination among organizations. Iowa State University, Publications Distribution. North Central Regional Extension Publication 80, 1979.

Nystrom, P. C., & Starbuck, W. H. (Eds.), *Prescriptive models of organizations.* New York: North-Holland, 1977.

Pfefer, J., & Salancik, G. R. *The external control of organizations.* New York: Harper and Row, 1978.

Schermerhorn, J. R., Jr. Determinants of interorganizational cooperation. *Academy of Management Journal,* 1975, *18,* 846–856.

Turk, H. *Organizations in modern life.* San Francisco: Jossey-Bass, 1977.

U.S. National Advisory Commission on Rural Poverty. *The people left behind.* Washington, D.C.: U.S. Government Printing Office, 1967, Chapter 10.

Warren, R. L. The interorganizational field as a focus for investigation. *Administrative Science Quarterly,* 1967, *12,* 396–419.

Warren, R. L. *The Community in America.* Chicago: Rand McNally, 1978.

Whetten, D. A. Towards a contingency model for designing interorganizational delivery systems. *Organization and Administrative Sciences,* 1977, *8,* 77–96.

Chapter 8

UNRESOLVED ISSUES AND PRIORITY
QUESTIONS FOR THE 1980s

Theoretical, Methodological, and Applied
Points of View

We have considered the merits of viewing community and community subsystems from an interorganizational relations (IOR) perspective. An IOR perspective complements other ways of conceptualizing the community and may also be quite helpful in conceptualizing multicounty units of social organization and relationships between local and higher ranking units.

We have summarized and integrated the available literature that focuses upon the nature and impact of IOR for particular organizations, dyads, and networks. We have also considered the importance of boundary spanning and the costs and benefits associated with boundary roles for the incumbents. Efforts have been made to emphasize results that have relevance for persons with applied interests. Finally, training materials available to orient and teach persons interested in community development have been described and evaluated.

It is one thing to trace the development of a perspective but quite another to predict its future. It is even more difficult to specify what should be done next in order to maximize a perspective's contribution. But that is exactly what this chapter is all about. Five persons who are quite actively involved in theory development, research, and applied work have been asked to read the previous chapters, consider the existing development of the IOR perspective, and specify what should be done next. For example, it is impossible to review IOR literature and not appreciate the theoretical contributions of Levine and White (1961) who specified exchange as a conceptual framework or of Thompson's (1967) classic book, *Organizations in Action*. Indeed, one might even suggest that relatively few real theoretical contributions have occurred in recent years. Too few of the empirical studies have really emphasized interorganizational dimensions but, instead, have emphasized the IOR of particular organizations. It is obvious too that relatively few specialists have been interested in the needs of applied persons, and a great deal needs to be done in terms of developing training materials and in designing training. Each of the persons who are sharing their views with us here have been asked to respond to two questions:

1. From your point of view, what are the major gaps within the IOR field that exist today?

2. What are the most important steps to be taken during the 1980s in order to meet unanswered needs and priority issues?

Are these persons prophets of doom, or are they optimistic? What does the future hold? Let's consider what they say.

NOTES ON THE ANALYSIS AND MEASUREMENT OF IOR
BY RICHARD H. HALL*

When Charles Mulford asked me to provide some comments on the state of the art in IOR research, I virtually leapt at the opportunity. Having recently completed (Morrissey, Hall, and Lindsey, 1981) a source book on the measurement of IOR and having received thoughtful criticisms of this effort, I felt that I

*Richard H. Hall is with the Department of Sociology, State University of New York at Albany.

was on top of the literature in the field. As always happens, second thoughts intervened between the initial feeling and the actual putting down of thoughts on paper. Third thoughts then entered as I reviewed what has been noted on the pages that precede these comments, since some of my concerns about the state of the IOR research art have been addressed. Nonetheless, I still see areas where practitioners and theorists alike have either ignored significant issues *or* appear to have reached premature closure.

The Environment

Contemporary organizational and IOR theory places a heavy emphasis on the environment. Chapter 3 of this volume contains an up-to-date account of the various analytical models proposed to conceptualized the environment. Unfortunately, we seem to stop there, with various conceptualizations of the environment based around resources and information.

We have been unable to translate these conceptualizations into meanings in terms of the operations of the organizations we study. At the same time, we have no real indication of what the exact impact of certain environmental conditions is on IOR. For example, does an unstable, turbulent environment contribute to conflict in a dyad, set, or network? Or, would such an environment contribute to increased coordination?

The problem is that we seem not to have asked the correct questions. I know of few IOR studies that have actually measured environmental conditions. Obviously, this is a difficult task, but certainly the emphasis on the environment demands that we at least try. Ideally, we should obtain evidence regarding environmental conditions and changes as we obtain evidence regarding IOR. Even if this were done, of course, there would be no proof that these conditions had anything to do with our observed IOR.

An alternative approach would be to ask our organizational respondents directly about their perceptions of the important environmental conditions and changes for their organizations. We should also ask them if and how these conditions and changes have affected their ongoing relationships with the other organizations with which we are concerned. The questions asked would have to be phrased in such a manner as to permit respondents to use their own definitions or conceptualizations of the environment. If this alternative were taken seriously, we could develop an empirically derived conceptualization of the environment, which may or may not coincide with the formulations in the literature.

There is another aspect of the environment of IOR particularly important for community development that has been overlooked. Communities seem to differ in the extent to which they are characterized by cleavages or hositilities based on factors such as race, ethnicity, and class. There also appear to be differences between communities in terms of the tradition of cooperation between public and private sectors and within these sectors. This should be taken into account in our analyses of IOR in these contexts.

Measurement

The state of the art in measuring IOR can be accurately described as undergoing development. Our work (Morrissey et al., 1981) reflects this as do several chapters in this volume. Development is occurring as investigators become aware of others' works and themselves attempt to develop more sophisticated instrumentation.

There is a potential roadblock in this development. Advanced analytical techniques may impede the development of IOR measures. Various forms of network analyses appear to be embraced prematurely. Most network analyses end up using a single measure of IOR. From this we see elegant descriptions with varying numbers of dimensions. Block modeling does reveal blocks of organizations with structurally equivalent positions in a network. Knowing this, what have we learned about their actual interactions? This is an unfair question, since network analysts are asking different questions. My fear is that these sophisticated techniques are being used for their own sake, without regard for their content. Data analysis techniques should be the servants of what has been measured and not an end in themselves.

Outcomes

This volume is one of the few IOR analyses that directly confronts the issue of the outcomes of IOR. Here the emphasis is on community development, with a heavy emphasis on co-ordination. I would like to see an alternative approach to outcomes developed for the field.

A concern with outcomes at the IOR level is analogous with interest in effectiveness at the organizational level. After reviewing the alternative approaches to effectiveness, I developed (Hall, 1982) a "contradiction" model of effectiveness. Without going into detail here, this model stresses contradictions among organizational goals and organizational constituents. The same approach might be useful in analyzing the outcomes of IOR.

Approaching IOR from a goal perspective, we can see social service organizations interacting, regardless of the basis of the interactions, for purposes of client change, client control, increased benefits, lowered costs, and improved information flows. On the face of it, lowered costs, increased benefits, and the other interaction goals appear to be contradictory. Movement toward one would inhibit movement toward another. This point is too seldom recognized in IOR analyses.

The same contradiction is evident in terms of the constituents of IOR. Again using social service organizations as the example, constituents would include clients, the significant others of clients, the staffs of the agencies involved, and the community-at-large. Each constituent group may have different desires regarding the outcome, with differences probably present within some of the identified groups.

These differences are undoubtedly settled in a political-economic context as has been suggested in this volume. Any settlement will be in favor of one set of constituents and one set of goals at the expense of others. The point being made here is that we should not lose sight of the multiplicity and contradictions present in goals and constituents.

SOME PREREQUISITES FOR APPLYING RESEARCH AND THEORY ON IOR
WITH EMPHASIS ON THE BUSINESS SECTOR
BY STEVE K. PAULSON*

Clearly, there is a necessity for developing applied social science tools in the form of design procedures and training materials in the IOR area. This is so not only because of organizational expansion in all community sectors that has forced the need for effective IOR but also because of increased demands placed on social scientists to become more "practical"—to be able to offer alternative solutions for immediate problems. The work by the Iowa State group (Klonglan Winkelpleck, Mulford, and Warren, 1975) is an excellent beginning in this area as is the work by Lauffer (1978) and Van de Ven and Ferry (1980). While this applied work should continue, it will be hampered by underdevelopment in the following areas:

1. literature syntheses;
2. research on public and nonprofit organizational interaction in the context of environmental information flows;
3. research on private business interaction in the context of environmental resource pools; and
4. research on IOR between public and private sectors in the community-wide context of both information flows and resource pools.

When one goes to the IOR literature with a very large net, the variety and amount of the catch is impressive. Virtually all of the social sciences are represented including, as the more prominent, management, marketing, sociology, anthropology, political science, economics, psychology, public health, criminology, and education. This range provides many unique concepts, methods, data and applications as well as the potential for

*Steve K. Paulson is with the Department of Business Administration, University of North Florida.

confusion through the use of different and vague terms for similar ideas. Work in synthesizing the literature would make ideas outside one's field more readily available and help to avoid the waste of duplicated research and semantic confusion. The present book is an illustration of this type of synthesizing work with the central topic of community development. Whetten (1981) provides another beginning point for synthesis in terms of IOR materials from four areas: public administration, marketing, economics, and sociology. Whetten (1981) categorizes this material according to typical organizations studied, which are service agencies, businesses, and all organizations of the community.

While IOR research has been conducted in all of these sectors, certain specific areas have been neglected. The distinction made by Aldrich (1979) between the environment as resource pools and as information flows is discussed earlier in the present book and is useful for pointing out these neglected areas especially when combined with Whetten's (1981) sector distinctions (see Figure 8-1).

Examples of the dominant type of research are interlocking directorates among business organizations in the private sector where IOR is a management tool used to provided access to information (cell B; cf. Allen, 1974) and joint programs among health and welfare organizations in the public sector where IOR

Figure 8-1. Nine Areas of Research and Theory on IOR

Nature of the Environment	Sector		
	Service agency (public/private nonprofit)	Business (private profit)	Community (public & private)
Information Flow	A**	B***	G*
Resource Pool	C***	D**	H*
Information and Resources	E*	F*	I*

*Severely neglected area of IOR theorizing and research
**Less frequent area of IOR theorizing and research
***Dominant area of IOR theorizing and research

is the consequence of resource scarcity in the environment regardless of managerial action (cell C; cf. Aiken and Hage, 1968). Examples of the less frequently studied forms of IOR are joint ventures among firms in highly concentrated industries (cell D; cf. Pfeffer and Nowak, 1976) and intense conflict among United Fund organizations over information control (cell A; cf. White, 1968).

The remaining "marginal" cells (E through I) represent areas where very little research has been conducted and hence very little applied work can be started. In addition, it would seem that research in these marginal areas would depend upon work done in areas represented by the nonmarginal "internal" cells. Thus, a research agenda might proceed from literature syntheses to underresearched internal topics to the marginal topics culminating in the most comprehensive research represented by cell I. The "business" sector is often (Hall, 1977; Whetten, 1981) referred to as being the least researched in terms of IOR and thus can be used as an appropriate illustration of this research agenda. The remainder of this statement is concerned with IOR research needs in the business sector.

Past research on business IOR can be found in a few monographs (Galaskiewicz, 1979; Gillespie and Mileti, 1979; Pennings, 1980) and anthologies (Evan, 1978; Nystrom and Starbuck, 1981; Tuite, Chisholm, and Radnor, 1972) and a variety of academic journals in the areas of labor and human relations, general sociology, rural and industrial sociology, applied psychology, management and administrative science, marketing and retailing, business, and economics. A variety of business IOR forms would be found including marketing (buying, selling) channels, joint ventures and subsidiaries, cartels and other interfirm organizations, mergers and divestitures, interlocking directorates, multidivisional and multinational relationships and various forms of market competition (cf. Reve and Stern, 1979). Business-nonbusiness IOR forms would also be found including interest group relations (environmental, political, etc.), governmental regulatory relations, philanthropic relations, media relations, and labor relations. Each form could be classified according to the cells of Figure 8-1 and then further classified in terms of the degree of cooperation and conflict present and the structural characteristics of the relationship itself (cf. Marrett, 1971). The most critical classification, however, would be in terms of the conception of the environment within which the IOR was studied (i.e., cell B, D, or F).

While most research on business organizational IOR has taken the view that the environment is intensely competitive, it is usually seen, at least for large organizations, as an entity to be managed by gaining access to critical information (cell B). Many strategies have been designed under the academic rubric of "organization theory" or "business policy" to gain such access, yet much remains to be learned about the actual effects of such strategies other than simply short-run sucess or failure in generating profit (Hayes and Abernathy, 1980). A more critical research need, however, is a focus on IOR among business organizations when the competitive environment is seen as an entity to fit one's organization into rather than as an entity that can be changed to fit the organization (cell D). Applications from this point of view have been developed, particularly for the small business, under the academic heading of "market identification" and "consumer behavior," although they have had limited conceptual scope.

Perhaps the most realistic approach, and the one in which the least amount of work has been done, is where the environment is thought of as consisting of both types (cell F). It is this complex, yet very realistic, view of the environment that offers the most payoff for social science applications in business IOR. Treating the environment as unilaterally one type or the other is too simplistic for most business organizations and could lead to inappropriate and quickly self-defeating IOR. The challenge to social science, then, is to specify conditions under which different organizational subunits, at specific points in time with specific objectives, should establish IOR under one or the other view of the environment. This challenge for developing such prescriptions can be met only after certain basic research and theorizing work has been done, and this has been the argument of this brief statement.

Clearly, in North America, success of organizational life will depend heavily on the effectiveness of IOR across and within sectors. And this effectiveness will depend, in part, upon the opportunity and motivation of social scientists to do the required basic research and theoretical work from which applied tools can be developed. With the possible exception of the business sector, and public sector regulation of business, the national climate is not encouraging as far as providing support for such work. One short-run social science strategy, then, would be to make extensive use of available literature and research findings through syntheses, conduct research only for the most critical tests and then, where appropriate, make use of the business sector as a relatively untapped source of information about IOR in the context of the larger community.

QUALITATIVE AND QUANTITATIVE METHODS IN INTERORGANIZATIONAL RESEARCH
BY JOSEPH J. MOLNAR*

Interorganizational research has been characterized by a predominantly quantitative and structural approach to the understanding of interorganizational networks. Relying primarily on survey modes of data collection, quantitative analysts have sought to determine an individual organization's level of interorganizational activity (Aiken and Hage, 1968; Rogers, 1974a) to explain bilateral relationships (Molnar and Rogers, 1979; Schermerhorn, 1975) and to discover properties of the network as a unit of analysis (Metcalfe, 1976; Turk, 1973).

Qualitative approaches to interorganizational research are less frequently encountered, but certainly Mott's (1968) study of a coordinating council, Warren's examination of war on poverty agencies (Warren et al., 1974), and Benson's (1975) political economy approach each illustrates observational and archival approaches to data collection. Qualitative analysts seek to identify and explore the broader—meaning structures that underly pat-

*Joseph J. Molnar is with the Department of Agricultural Economics and Rural Sociology, Auburn University.

terns of avoidance, conflict, and cooperation in interorganizational networks.

This section makes some assertations about the character and trend of previous interorganizational studies. It also seeks to identify some neglected or emerging aspects of research on relationships between organizations and the character of interorganizational networks. We examine quantitative trends, qualitative developments, and conclude with some recommendations for future research.

Quantitative Approaches

Interorganizational research is broadly conceived as an effort to predict, explain, and understand relationships between organizations. Dependent variables often include recorded incidents, reports of contacts, frequency of contacts, nature of contacts, perceptions of relations, and evaluations of the effectiveness, prestige, or potency of alter organizations (see Morrissey et al., 1981). Assessments of conflict, cooperation, and responsiveness have been used to quantify and understand interorganizational activity (Hall, Clark, Giordano, Johnson, and Van Roeker, 1977; Thomas, Walton, and Dutton, 1972). In addition, interorganizational variables have been used to understand intraorganizational processes (Rogers and Molnar, 1976).

As White's (1974) review points out, intra- and interorganizational studies share a lot in common but each also presents characteristic difficulties. When interorganizational dyads or relationships are the unit of analysis, discrepant reports or perceptions of the relationship become problematic (Molnar, 1978; 1980; Paulson, 1976). Accounting for intransitive assessment of shared experience, structure, or commitment may require methodological as well as substantive explanations.

Using survey data to summarize dyadic relationships or map entire networks places heavy reliance on the reliability and validity of the data collection procedures (Carmines and Zeller, 1979). The use of difference scores and an often unwarranted reliance on interrater reliability may jeopardize the effective use of the powerful statistical tools that have been fruitfully applied in other settings (Cronbach, 1958; Cronbach and Gleser, 1953). Thus, the combination of individual survey reports to summarize relationships presents a distinct challenge to the creativity and resourcefulness of the quantitative analyst.

Properties of dyadic ties include symmetry, reciprocity, multiplexity, strength, direct or indirect linkage, and structural equivalence (Lincoln, 1980). Others have shown that interorganizational relationships differ by hierarchial level in the organization (Klonglan, Warren, Winkelpleck, and Paulson, 1976). The wide range of measurement properties of dyadic relationships illustrates the difficulty of parsimoniously conceptualizing and measuring interorganizational processes. We seem to lack clear and consistent conceptual frameworks that organize available measures and anticipate additional dimensions of interorganizational linkages.

Another genre of quantitative analysis in interorganizational research relates to the properties of networks (Burt, 1980; Lincoln, 1980). Various techniques have been fruitfully employed to examine interlocking directorates (Pennings, 1980), centrality of organizations (Rogers, 1974b), and the consequences of weak or indirect ties between groups (Granovetter, 1973). Burt's (1977) work has greatly advanced the theoretical and methodical sophistication of this avenue of activity, but it remains at a high level of abstraction and there has been limited success at translating the practical or administrative consequences of this knowledge. One contribution that remains to be made is the linkage of these seemingly powerful techniques to the world of policy and interorganizational design for service delivery, program coordination, or regulatory efficiency (Van de Ven, et al., 1974; 1976).

Network properties include: density of ties, connectivity, clustering, hierarchy, and the centrality of individual units relative to the network. The methodology of block modeling has been employed to algebraically summarize networks as systems of role relationships across multiple domains of content (Boorman and White, 1976). Block modeling is used to identify structurally equivalent sets of actors, that is, those who have similar patterns of linkage to other groups. Here again, the challenge lies in expanding the substantive utility of mathematically sophisticated techniques.

Qualitative Approaches

Qualitative approaches to interorganizational research attempt to discover, explore, and convey the social-psychological paradigms that govern perception, conduct, and reaction in interorganizational settings. Their contributions lie in exposing the rules, understandings, and conceptualizations that govern the world of social activity in various organizational contexts.

Ethnographic or participant observation methods are used to examine the acts, activities, meanings, modes of participation, relationships, and settings of interorganizational activity (Lofland, 1974). Van Maanen's (1979) work on urban policing shows the use of participant observation, informal interviewing, document collecting, and other techniques to gain an in-depth understanding of organizational phenomena. Although many studies employ those techniques as entry points or pilot works for quantitative studies, few explore the full interplay between archival evidence, intensive interviewing, and observational data (Jick, 1979; Sieber, 1973).

Qualitative techniques have a distinct role to play in the formulation, design, and conduct of interorganizational research (Scott, 1965). Qualitative studies often suffer from a limited ability to generalize and the extended burdens of on-site activity required of the researcher (Miles, 1979). Unfortunately, consumers of interorganizational research often must be assuaged of doubts as to the objectivity and value of narrative reports that lack the authority of seeming numerical precision and the often exaggerated prestige of statistical analysis.

Challenge to Interorganizational Research

Interorganizational research questions will increasingly demand longitudinal analysis to discover cycles, phases, and variable modes of participation in interorganizational relationships (Kimberly and Miles, 1980). Research designs will increasingly resemble a "hull" of interwoven quantitative and qualitative data collection efforts that will be combined to provide a deeper, extended understanding of interorganizational phenomena (Cronbach, 1980). Measurement of interorganizational activity will likely broaden to encompass the wide range of potential exchanges between organizations and employ archival and computerized records as sources of unobtrusive indicators (Flaherty, Barry, and Swift, 1978).

The impetus to study interorganizational networks will likely take on more explicitly applied motivations, seeking to understand the dynamics, structures, and processes underlying various policy outcomes (Molnar and Rogers, 1982), level of interorganizational response to problem situations (Turk, 1973), and the intermesh of activity within and between levels of government (Bardach, 1977).

The challenge to all interorganizational researchers will be to increase the reliability and validity of their data, to undertake multiple modes of data collection, and to select theoretically meaningful problems that contribute to an administrative constituency who can use the research findings. Thus the conceptual framework, data collection techniques, and analytic methods chosen must be more systematic, rigorous, and meaningful to researchers as well as applied audiences.

INCREASING IOR'S CONTRIBUTION TO COMMUNITY DEVELOPMENT
BY VERNON D. RYAN*

Speaking from the standpoint of a community development specialist as opposed to one whose expertise is in IOR, I can assure you that we are in need of practical theories to guide purposive action programs. In time, the IOR perspective as outlined by Mulford may prove to be an invaluable orientation to satisfy this need. Personally, I believe the potential is there, but a major shift in the focus of IOR research may be necessary if its con-

*Vernon D. Ryan is with the Department of Sociology, Iowa State University.

tribution to the practice of community development is to be realized. In the following paragraphs, some personal thoughts on present shortcomings and suggested changes in IOR research are presented.

Community development refers to action purposively directed toward altering community structure in a positive way (Wilkinson, 1972, p.45). From an IOR perspective, community structure is seen as recurring relations and dependencies among organizations. Thus, community development pertains to attempts to alter these interrelationships for the benefit of the entire unit.

Assuming reasonable accuracy in my assessment of IOR's approach to community development, I call attention to what appears to be a disparity in orientations between IOR and community development. Specifically, when community structure is limited to IOR, there is a tendency for IOR to overlook the broader goals and strategies of community development. Interorganizational relations, with its genesis in organizational theory, traditionally examines the influence of IOR on participating organizations. Even in studies of environments, the emphasis usually is on information and resources to be utilized by organizations *for their own benefit*. Therefore, what we end up knowing is more about the performance of organizations.

Albeit rich in tradition and valuable for the accumulation of knowledge, the conventional orientation of IOR falls short of community development, which is broader in orientation than organizations and their relationships. Take, for example, the areas of community leadership or the formation of local coalitions. As critical concerns of community development, these traits may be closely associated with measures of structure not affiliated with IOR. Therefore, if the basic orientation of IOR is to move away from organizations and toward the broader concerns of community development, an alternative definition of community structure is needed that is inclusive of community development's goals and strategies. Community as seen from an interactionist perspective provides us with such an orientation.

Briefly, community defined from an interactionist perspective sees structure in process and process in structure by calling attention to the patterns of relations (actions) among individuals (actors) and organizations (associations) when dealing with local opportunities and problems (Kaufman, 1959). In fact, these three—actions, actors, associations—are treated as basic elements of community structure and process. Process is found in specific relationships between local individuals and organizations. But process turns to structure, analytically speaking, when relationships become regularized and routinized. New structural properties of the community emerge out of recurring relationship patterns.

With this brief overview of an interactionist perspective of community, we now turn to the importance of IOR in community development. At the community level, we find two types of organizations. The first type includes organizations which are primarily service oriented. These organizations create new services, provide existing services more efficiently, and utilize available resources to the satisfaction of local residents. As measures of performance, profit and efficiency are primary considerations. Previous research in IOR has been particularly useful in helping to better understand this type of organization.

The second type of community organization has received less attention. Rather than drawing attention to its own performance and outputs, these organizations are more concerned with coordinating the activities of organizations of the first type in order to preserve the identity of the entire community. They are more community oriented, as opposed to organization oriented, since their goals are more consistent with what is needed at the broader community level.

To facilitate community development, IOR needs to focus on the interaction between these two types of organizations. For instance, we presently know very little about the possible integration or conflict between the organizational goals of the two types. Interorganizational relations could also assist in the development of strategies that could be adopted by the coordinative organizations when working with service-oriented organizations. Both are needed in any community, but since one is service oriented while the other is more coordinative oriented, we need to better understand the causes and consequences of alternative relationship patterns so that the goals of community development might be achieved.

In closing, I see great potential in the application of IOR in community development efforts. To reach this potential, however, IOR needs to shift its orientation away from organizational behavior and toward a community level of analysis. One way of doing this is to take an interactionist perspective of community. In doing so, a broader definition of community structure is offered which includes all forms of relationship patterns, i.e., between individuals as well as organizations, and also incorporates community development strategies into the framework since structures (as goals) are seen as emergent properties of process (as strategies). In my judgment, such a change in emphasis would dramatically increase IOR's contribution to community development.

BRIDGING THE GAP GAP BETWEEN COORDINATION KNOWLEDGE AND APPLICATION
BY BETTY L. WELLS*

The potential utility of knowledge of interorganizational coordination for community development practitioners has been established in the previous chapters. This potential holds whether one views community development primarily as an endeavor to strengthen horizontal linkages within a community, vertical linkages between communities and hierarchical levels, or the simultaneous development of both sets of relations. However, from an applied point of view, there are gaps which prevent the IOR field from realizing its potential for community development. Some of these gaps have to do with our knowledge base, others with application. Problems inherent in the application of knowledge about interorganizational coordination have received less attention, but they are obstacles of which any community development practitioner should be aware. Some knowledge prob-

*Betty L. Wells is with the Sociology Department, Iowa State University.

lems, some practical and ethical problems of application, and some strategies for approaching these problems will be outlined.

Despite its relevancy, I believe the IOR knowledge base is infrequently tapped. Discussions with community development practitioners provide insight into some of the reasons. Some practitioners have not received training and are thus unaware. Others find the literature to be highly abstract and difficult to operationalize in their communities. Still others (myself included) appreciate the potential value of this approach and use it frequently but are overwhelmed by seemingly infinite contingencies.

The first two knowledge problems, awareness and accessibility, have straightforward remedies (at least in principle)—the development of training materials, the implementation of training programs for community development professionals, and the applications of this knowledge in communities. My observations tend to confirm the conclusions drawn in some detail in Chapter 7. For this reason, the present discussion will focus on a third knowledge problem that stems from complexity: multiple contingencies.

Ideally, before becoming involved in a coordination program, community developers should attempt to assess factors such as barriers to coordination, the potential for successful outcome, and the costs and benefits for participating organizations. In this regard, the contingency model approach outlined by Whetten (1977) offers much promise. But in community development work, one quickly confronts the "real world." Despite the right (theoretical) combination of contextual contingencies that should lead to cooperation among community organizations, reality often asserts itself in the form of idiosyncratic conditions, difficult people, and miscommunication.

The contingency model is a first attempt and its assumptions are to be treated as hypotheses subject to empirical test (Whetten, 1977). Nonetheless, the number of contingencies may become overwhelming. If we consider only one contextual dimension in the contingency model—control over resources—an abundant/scarce dichotomy is really not very useful. Whetten (1977) acknowledges that both abundance and scarcity give rise to coordination problems. A review of previous chapters suggests some other dimensions of resources we should consider: complementarity of resource needs, external control of resources, alternative sources of resources, concentration of resources, number of external suppliers of resources, essentiality of resources, and competition for scarce resources. Because there are so many dimensions, which are not necessarily independent, interpreting these contingencies becomes quite complex. Such ambiguity makes it unlikely that practitioners will be able to treat resources in the straightforward manner suggested by the contigency model.

Despite this confusion, I am less troubled by knowledge gaps than by potential problems in the application of this knowledge. Some application problems would persist even in the absence of knowledge gaps. They derive from an uncritical acceptance of the benefits of coordination described variously in terms of increased resource utilization, efficiency, effectiveness, reduction of waste and duplication of services, synergism, mobilization potential, and the development of community capacity. In view of such promises, a practitioner may become so "sold" on coordination as to downplay its limitations. For both practical and ethical reasons, the community development practitioner must be careful not to overstate the benefits of coordination.

Let's look first at some practical reasons for caution. First of all, individuals and organizations do not always benefit from coordination. Warren (1970) argues that there are cases where clients would be best served by competition between agencies and that an emphasis on increased coordination between existing programs directs attention away from better programs. Whetten (1977) reminds us that extensive internal integration may reduce a system's ability to adapt, a potential liability in an unstable environment. In reality, only rarely will all organizations, and even less frequently all organizational members, benefit equally from coordination.

Second, complete coordination, even if desirable, is probably not possible short of merging two organizations. When more than two organizations are involved in a voluntary coordination effort, the complexities are such that coordination will be even more imperfect. A coordination field is something like a jigsaw puzzle with missing pieces.

Third, coordination may fail despite the best efforts of

practitioner and community participants. In such cases, benefits derive from the coordination process rather than the coordination product. If communication has been initiated and a dialog established, the process may result in increased community capacity and enhance future coordination efforts.

Fourth, the development, operation, and maintenance costs of coordination can be extremely high. In many cases, it costs more in time, energy, and organizational complexity to coordinate activities than it would to continue operations as usual. At least in the short run, and for some organizations more than others, the costs of coordination may outrun the benefits.

Practitioners should also be aware of potential ethical dilemmas. In cases of hierarchically mandated coordination, the practitioner may become identified with the hierarcy. He or she may face a loss of credibility or become a potential scapegoat. This is especially troublesome when a mandate results in the elimination of local jobs or otherwise reduces local autonomy.

Even in the less controversial situation of locally initiated and controlled coordination, it is unlikely that all organizations will benefit equally. Most locally initiated coordination efforts are undertaken because no single organization has adequate resources (usually money) with which to solve a community problem. And since mandates are not the exclusive property of extralocal hierarchies (as indicated by the case study of locally mandated coordination in Chapter 6), it is possible that some organizations may lose a great deal.

Practitioners should also consider the question, "Who benefits?" If we speak of community development in a broad sense, we would hope that the entire community would benefit. However, if the practitioner works to educate members of a specific organization on coordination strategies and options, the community is not necessarily the beneficiary. In a more ideal situation, where the client is a set of organizations, it is still possible that one organizational set may benefit at the expense of another. There is a related question, "Which communities?" A potential paradox is that those communities most in need of coordination assistance and capacity building may be less likely to receive assistance than those with more abundant resources and the ability to utilize external assistance (Lorenz, 1981).

There are no easy solutions, only practical approaches, to problems in applying coordination knowledge. One piece of advice is for practitioners to anticipate potential problems when planning coordination programs. For example, community development practitioners should maintain their identities by clearly articulating roles and responsibilities. They should provide a balanced presentation of the costs as well as the benefits of coordination, differences between locally and hierarchically initiated coordination, and between voluntary and mandated coordination. When possible, practitioners should work with organizational sets (rather than single organizations) over an extended period of time.

It is unlikely that the present trend toward increased coordination and integration will subside any time soon. The argument may be made that integration (and disintegration) is a natural process we may facilitate but is nonetheless inevitable. If so, the community development professional must be equipped with an arsenal of practical skills and the very best knowledge base. It is here that the researcher and practitioner can be of assistance to each other.

Several well-developed models and theories have been presented in this book. Conclusive tests of these models and theories will require much additional empirical research. We may lack research funds, but unfortunately we do not lack opportunities to gather data. Communities are natural laboratories for observing the organizational consequences of shifts in environmental contexts. As a field of investigation, IOR is in the rather enviable position of being able to investigate changing community structures from a theoretically informed perspective. As a consequence, our research need not be designed for exploratory purposes, as is so often the case, but can instead be designed to test hypotheses. It should be possible to avoid the haphazard accumulation of piecemeal empirical studies.

For this optimistic research scenario to be realized, the existing theoretical (and empirical) literature must be made accessible to community development practitioners. These people have abundant opportunities to do field work in these natural laboratories, usually at the request and with the cooperation of communities. Indeed, if rumors of a new federalism come to pass, we may be awash in a sea of data. Of course, documentation of these field experiments is critical.

As an example, case studies prepared by practitioners with adequate training and knowledge of the IOR literature would allow us to compile data and test contingency theory. As we know, the contigency model offers the promise of matching the characteristics of unique community contexts with an appropriate level of integration. However, it is one thing to say that different contexts can support varying degrees of interorganizational coordination and quite another to specify these contexts in a practically meaningful way.

When are environments really different? Environmental specifications in the organizational literature are so ambiguous as to be nearly worthless. Task environments are quite specific but economic or political conditions constitute general environments shared by entire regions or even countries. One useful strategy might be to greatly expand the contexts from which we approach organizational coordination. Cross-cultural investigations would offer a great variation in contexts and could serve as a most basic test of the contingency model. The variation of contexts over time would be another telling comparison. Since this literature was established in a period of relatively abundant resources and has continued to develop through times of relative resource scarcity, some useful bench marks have been established.

Theories are being tested everyday in communities. The opportunities are encouraging, but missed opportunities are distressing. The coordination literature suggests that this is the time for students of social organization to coordinate the efforts of the theoreticians, methodologists, applied scientists, and practitioners among us for the best scientific payoff.

SUMMARY

The remarks of the five specialists are both provocative and enlightening. Each person is at least somewhat optimistic about the further development and maturity of an IOR perspective, but each is also aware of obstacles that must be overcome.

The first three specialists are primarily concerned about our inadequate conceptualization of IOR and with inadequate methodologies. It is obvious from the remarks of Hall and Paulson that the environments of organizations will continue to be a focus of our attention. Hall points out that we need to better translate conceptualizations of the environment into meanings in terms of the operations of organizations. We also need to better understand how exactly various kinds of environments contribute to exchanges and/or conflict between organizations. Paulson calls for a more complex view of environments and effectively uses his typology of environments and organizational sectors to point out research needs and priorities. Because past work has emphasized research with service agencies and with community organizations, learning much more about the IOR of organizations in the business sector is a high priority.

Hall, Paulson, and Molnar call for better measurement and more complete methodologies. Molnar's challenge to specialists to better use both qualitative and quantitative tools may prove difficult for those who have not used eclectic approaches. Qualitative approaches, especially studies based upon participant observation, are, however, badly needed because of the insights they promise. In addition, Molnar's suggestion that better use should be made of archival and available computerized records as unobtrusive measures of IOR activity is excellent.

Each of these specialists, but especially Ryan and Wells, realizes that an IOR perspective will never fully develop unless much more concern is given to studying meaningful problems that contribute directly to the needs of applied audiences. Ryan is certainly correct in his criticism of IOR work and its lack of direct application to community development. Ryan hopes that we will take a broader perspective, away from a concern for particular organizations and their IOR, toward a community level of analysis.

Wells is quite direct and right on target in her discussion of gaps that presently prevent the IOR perspective from reaching its potential for community development. Her discussion of knowledge gaps, the limitations of coordination, and of ethical problems of application is very relevant. Wells' call for IOR specialists to better utilize communities as natural laboratories for analyzing shifts in environmental contexts and to better utilize community development specialists as partners in these efforts cannot be ignored. Her discussion of the gains to be realized from studies conducted in different cultural settings is also most relevant.

We have explored here the advantages to be gained from an IOR perspective. We have learned much about the strategies used by particular organizations to manage their environments and the factors that influence the interaction between organizations. In addition, we are better equipped to understand the activation of networks of organizations and the outcomes of collective efforts. These concerns are not merely academic but have great practical importance. Government leaders concerned about inflation, competition for available resources, and possible program duplication call for greater understanding of coordination at all levels of government. Business leaders and agency administrators recognize that their operations cannot be separated from the interorganizational context within which they exist. The question isn't whether or not an IOR perspective is needed, but whether or not these needs will be met.

Hopefully, the issues raised in this chapter and the priorities suggested for further work will be taken into consideration by specialists who are committed to the more complete development of an IOR perspective.

REFERENCES

Aiken, M., & Hage, J. Organizational interdependence and intraorganizational structure. *American Sociological Review*, 1968, *33*, 912–930.

Aldrich, H. E. *Organizations and environment*. Englewood Cliffs, NJ: Prentice-Hall, 1979.

Allen, M. P. The structure of interorganizational elite cooptation: Interlocking corporate directorates. *American Sociological Review*, 1974, *39*, 393–406.

Bardach, E. *The implementation game*. Cambridge, MA: MIT Press, 1977.

Benson, J. K. The interorganizational network as a political economy. *Administrative Science Quarterly*, 1975, *20*, 199–249.

Boorman, S. A., & White, H. C. Social structures from multiple networks. *American Journal of Sociology*, 1976, *81*, 1384–1446.

Burt, R. S. Power in a social typology. *Social Science Research*, 1977, *6*, 1–83.

———Models of network structure. *Annual Review of Sociology*, 1980, *6*, 79–141.

Carmines, E., & Zeller, R., *Reliability and validity assessment*. Beverly Hills, CA: Sage Publications, Inc., 1979.

Cronbach, L. J. Proposals leading to analytic treatment of social perception scores. In R. Tajiuri & L. Petrullo (Eds.), *Person perception and interpersonal behavior*. Stanford, CA: Stanford University Press, 1958, pp. 353–379.

Cronbach, L. J. & Gleser, G. C. Assessing similarity between profiles. *Psychological Bulletin*, 1953, *50*, 457–473.

Cronbach, L. J. *Toward reform of program evaluation*. San Francisco: Jossey-Bass, 1980.

Evan, W. M. *Interorganizational relations*. Philadelphia: University of Pennsylvania Press, 1978.

Flaherty, E. W., Barry, E., & Swift, M. Use of an unobtrusive measure for the evaluation of interagency coordination. *Evaluation Quarterly*, 1978, *2*, 261–273.

Galaskiewicz, J. *Exchange networks and community politics*. Beverly Hills, CA: Sage Publications, Inc., 1979.

Gillespie, D. F., & Mileti, D. S., *Technostructures and interorganizational relations*. Lexington, MA: D.C. Heath and Company, 1979.

Granovetter, M. The strength of weak ties. *American Journal of Sociology*, 1973, *78*, 1360–1380.

Hall, R. H. *Organizations: Structure and process*. Englewood Cliffs, NJ: Prentice-Háll, 1977.

———*Organizations: Structure and process*, 3rd ed. Englewood Cliffs, NJ: Prentice-Hall, 1982.

Hall, R. H., Clark, J. P., Giordano, P. C., Johnson, P. V., Van Roeker, M. Patterns of interorganizational relationships. *Administrative Science Quarterly*, 1977, *22*, 457–474.

Hayes, R. H., & Abernathy, W. J. Managing our way to economic decline. *Harvard Business Review*, 1980, *58*, 67–77.

Jick, T. D. Mixing qualitative and quantitative methods: triangulation in action. *Administrative Science Quarterly*, 1979, *24*, 602–611.

Kaufman, H. F. Toward an interactional conception of community. *Social Forces*, 1959, *38*, 8–17.

Klonglan, G. E., Warren, R. D., Winkelpleck, J. M., & Paulson, S. K. Interorganizational measurement in the social services sector: Differences by hierarchical level. *Administrative Science Quarterly*, 1976, *21*, 675–87.

Klonglan, G.E., Winkelpleck, J. M., Mulford C. L., & Warren, R. D. *Creating interorganizational coordination: Instructor's guide.* Department of Sociology, Iowa State University, Ames, Iowa: Sociology Report No. 122C, 1975.

Kimberly, J. R. & Miles, R. H. *The organizational life cycle.* San Francisco: Jossey-Bass, 1980.

Lauffer, A. *Social planning at the community level.* Englewood Cliffs, NJ: Prentice-Hall, 1978.

Levine, S., & White, P. E. Exchange as a conceptual framework for the study of interorganizational relationships. *Administrative Science Quarterly*, 1961, *5*, 583–610.

Lincoln, J. R. Intra- (and Inter-) organizational networks. In S. Bacharach (Ed.), *Perspectives in organizational sociology.* Greenwich, CT: JAI Press, 1980.

Lofland, J. *Analyzing social settings.* Belmont, CA: Wadsworth, 1974.

Lorenz, F. O. *City utilization of regional council technical assistance.* Unpublished Ph.D. dissertation, Iowa State University, Ames, IA, 1981.

Marrett, C. E. On the specification of interorganizational dimensions. *Sociology and Social Research*, 1971, *56*, 83–99.

Metcalfe, J. L. Organizational strategies and interorganizational networks. *Human Relations*, 1976, *29*, 327–343.

Miles, M. B. Qualitative data as an attractive nuisance: The problem of analysis. *Administrative Science Quarterly*, 1979, *24*, 590–601.

Morrissey, J. P., Hall, R. H., & Lindsey, M. L., *Interorganizational relations: A sourcebook of measures for mental health programs.* Albany: New York State Office of Mental Health 12229, 1981.

Molnar, J. J., Comparative organizational properties and interorganizational interdependence. *Sociology and Social Research*, 1978, *63*, 24–48.

———Measurement of dyadic properties. *Rural Sociology*, 1980, *42*, 268–269.

Molnar, J. J., & Rogers, D. L. A comparative model of interorganizational conflict. *Administrative Science Quarterly*, 1979, *24*, 205–245.

———Interorganizational coordination in environmental management: Process, strategy, and objective. In D. R. Mann (Ed.), *Implementation of environmental policy*, Lexington, MA: Lexington Books, 1982.

Mott, B. J. *Anatomy of a coordinating council.* Pittsburgh: University of Pittsburgh Press, 1968.

Nystrom, P. C., Starbuck, W. H. *Handbook of organizational design, Volume 1, adapting organizations to their environments.* New York: Oxford University Press, 1981.

Paulson, S. K. A theory and comparative analysis of interorganizational dyads. *Rural Sociology*, 1976, *41*, 311–330.

Pennings, J. M. *Interlocking directorates.* San Francisco: Jossey-Bass, 1980.

Pfeffer, J., & Nowak, P. Joint ventures and interorganiational interdependence. *Administrative Science Quarterly*, 1976, *21*, 398–418.

Reve, T., & Stern, L. W. Interorganizational relations in marketing channels. *Academy of Management Review*, 1979, *4*, 405–416.

Rogers, D. L. Towards a scale of interorganizational relations among public agencies. *Sociology and Social Research*, 1974a, *59*, 61–70.

———Sociometric analysis of interorganizational relations: Application of theory and measurement. *Rural Sociology*, 1974b, *39*, 487–503.

Rogers D. L., & Molnar, J. J. Organizational antecedents of role conflict and ambiguity in top level administrators. *Administrative Science Quarterly*, 1976, *21*, 598–610.

Schermerhorn, J. R. Determinants of interorganizational cooperation. *Academy of Management Journal*, 1975, *18*, 846–856.

Scott, W. R. Field methods in the study of organizations. Chapter 6 in J. G. March (Ed.), *Handbook on organizations*. New York: Rand McNally, 1965.

Sieber, S. On the integration of fieldwork and survey methods. *American Journal of Sociology*, 1973, *78*, 1335–1359.

Thomas, K. W., Walton, R. E., & Dutton, J. M. Determinants of inter-departmental conflict. In M. Tuite (Ed.), *Interorganizational decision-making*. Chicago: Aldine, 1972, pp.45–69.

Thompson, J. D. *Organizations in action*. New York: McGraw-Hill, 1967.

Tuite, M., Chisholm, R., & Radnor, M. *Interorganizational decision-making*. Chicago: Aldine, 1972.

Turk, H. *Interorganizational activation in urban communities: Deductions from the concept of system*. Washington, DC: American Sociological Association (Rose Monograph Series), 1973.

Van De Ven, A. H. On the nature, formation, and maintenance of relations among organizations. *Academy of Management Review*, 1976, *9*, 24–36.

Van De Ven, A. H., Emmett, D. C., & Koenig, R., Jr. Frameworks for interorganizational analysis. *Organization and Administrative Science*, 1974, *5*, 113–122.

Van De Ven, A. H., & Ferry, D. L. *Measuring and assessing organizations*. New York: John Wiley and Sons, 1980.

Van Maanen, J. The fact of fiction in organizational ethnography. *Administrative Science Quarterly*, 1979, *24*, 539–550.

Warren, R. L. Alternative strategies of inter-agency planning. In G. Ulasak (Ed.), *Inter-organizational research in health conference proceedings*, The John Hopkins University. HEW. PHS Publication National Center for Health Services Research and Development, 1970.

Warren, R. L., Rose, S. M., & Bergunder, A. F., *The structure of urban reform*. Lexington, MA: D.C. Heath and Company, 1974.

Whetten, D. A. Toward a contingency model for designing interorganizational service delivery systems. *Organization and Administrative Sciences*, 1977, *8*, 77–96.

————Interorganizational relations: A review of the field. *Journal of Higher Education*, 1981, *52*, 1–28.

White, P. E. Myth and reality in interorganizational behavior: A study of competition between two national voluntary health agencies. *American Journal of Public Health*, 1968, *58*, 289–304.

————Intra- and inter-organizational studies: Do they require separate conceptualizations? *Administration and Society*, 1974, *6*, 107–155.

Wilkinson, K. P. A field-theory perspective for community development research. *Rural Sociology*, 1972, *37*, 43–52.

Author Index

Key Word Index